Paul Watkins

How to be a big fish

How some professional service providers make more money than others

Paul Watkins

Paul Watkins

Published by Paul Watkins
Hamilton, New Zealand

First published 2009
Revised 2014

© **Paul Watkins 2009**
www.paulwatkins.co.nz

The right of Paul Watkins to be identified as the author of this work in terms of section 96 of the Copyright Act 1994 is hereby asserted.

All rights reserved. No part of this publication may be reproduced, stored in or introduced into a retrieval system, or transmitted, in any form or by any means (electronic, mechanical, recording or otherwise) without the prior written permission of the publisher.

ISBN 10 1502590387
ISBN 13 9781502590381

How to be a big fish

For Karen

Paul Watkins

Contents

Introduction	**3**
1 Three important points	**5**
First, a really big POINT	5
Next, a really big WORD	6
Now, the FISH bit	6
2 Why you must aim to be the big fish (in your field)	**7**
Who makes more, a GP or a specialist	7
How much would you pay for 'best of breed'?	8
Let's look at the relative sales of similar products in a highly competitive market	10
Why you should never be in the middle	11
The meaning of 'in your field'	13
3 The rise and rise and rise of the niche	**15**
Words from the master	15
The Long Tail	16
A TV Channel for food lovers	18
The death of the one-size-fits-all offer	18
Bloatware and Feature Creep	19
Feature Creep is alive in professional services	20
Depth of range is a fallacy	20
4 If you don't find a niche you won't be able to grow	**23**
How come your growth flattened out	23
Graph clients against cumulative business	24

5	**Who do you really, really want as clients?**	**29**
	Do some clients annoy you?	29
	Two questions to ask prospective clients	30
	Reactive versus proactive	30
	Pick your favourites	31
	There is no such thing as B2B marketing	33
	Let's go back to why you are doing this chart	34
6	**How to become the big fish in your chosen field**	**37**
	Procrustean Strategies	37
	Porter's 3 competitive strategies	38
	There can be only one	38
7	**Using PRICE as a strategy**	**41**
	Being a price leader	41
	The $5 milkshake	42
	Fixed price service	43
8	**Using a point of DIFFERENTIATION**	**45**
	How are you slightly different?	45
	Imply that your competitors do the opposite	46
	What is your point of difference?	46
	We pride ourselves on our service	48
	Why 'good service' is not a competitive edge	49
9	**Using FOCUS as a strategy**	**51**
	Choosing a focus	51
	Becoming world famous in one city block	52

You can have more than one at once	52
Financial advisors who focus with pinpoint accuracy	54
"But how can I deal with competing clients?"	55
I'm sorry that's outside my field of expertise...	55
Invent your own category	57

10 Do you have a brand or just a name — 61

"We always buy XX peanut butter, because it tastes so much better"	61
Is your brand good enough	62
First consider NOT changing your brand	62
It's the first letters of all our names	63
My name's spelled 'Luxury Yacht'...	63
CBE, ADW, IBM, CNW, CNN, CUA, UPS	64
It's all about me	64
Waddington Smyth and Bladdersworth	65
Where everyone gets a bargain	66
Places, loaded words and descriptors	66
I deal with Jack but John wrote to me	67
What about 'member of...' type brands	68
In summary	69

11 What marketing stuff works and what doesn't? — 71

The mathematics of marketing	71
Only half my advertising works, but which half?	72
The $$$ and ttt columns	74
It's a balancing act	74

12 The expensive stuff — 77

The bottom of the 'what works' chart	77

Two ways to find a new husband/wife	77
Don't let your ego do the talking	79
www.clichés-r-us.com	80
You can expect rain on Sunday	81
Should you advertise at all?	82
But what about the phone directories?	82
Ignore the Internet at your peril	83
Why your website may be a waste of time	84
Content is king	85
Creating great content	85
Search Engine Optimization	86
Finding a competent web designer	87
Audi vs BMW	87
Cold calling	88
13 Now the stuff that matters	**91**
The stuff in the middle	91
She's in the paper, she must be the expert!	91
Remember to reduce the size of the pond	92
They need you as much as you need them	93
Approaching your targeted media	93
Don't sell – educate!	94
Are your pens aircraft-safe?	95
Tell me why, not what	96
Tell me a story	97
Where do they congregate?	100
Some of the mechanics of speaking	100
I'm attending a course on the subject	103
Remember it's all about trust	103

14 Talk to the ones you already know — **105**
   The low hanging fruit — 105
   The magic of 90 day contact — 107
   Increased contact = Increase sales — 107
   Quarterly newsletters can do it — 108
   It could well be just a timing issue — 109

15 Referrals — **111**
   The difference between good and great advisers — 111
   Never ask a C-client for a referral — 111
   The hard task of asking for referrals — 112
   Referral 'rules of engagement' — 112
   Why don't you tip every waiter — 113
   So why is John so successful? — 115
   Who exactly are you asking for? — 115
   How do 2,350 other professionals do it? — 116
   Networking clubs — 117
   A seminar designed to attract referrals — 118
   Never waste a lunch — 121
   A client from your target niche — 121
   Other worthwhile lunch dates — 121
   It's a small world after all — 124
   The six degrees of separation — 125
   Making the six degrees work for you — 126
   How do you pay for a referral? — 126
   A subtle – yet surprisingly effective way — 127

16 Referrals from other professional service firms   **129**
    Find others with the same type of clientbase   129
    Form a 'Tight 5'   131
    They don't know what you do and may hate it   132
    Keep the third party informed   133
    WIIFT   134
    Joint seminars   134

17 The not so final word   **137**
    Being average doesn't work   137

"The mass market is dying. There is no longer one best song or one best kind of coffee. Now there are a million micro markets, but each micro market still has a BEST. If your micro market is 'organic markets in Tulsa', then that's your world. And being the best in THAT world is the place to be."

Seth Godin, internationally respected marketer, speaker and author. www.sethgodin.com

Paul Watkins

Introduction

If a friend said to you "I promise to do that for you", do you believe them? That entirely depends on how much you trust them of course, which is based on previous experiences and their reputation for keeping promises.

Selling professional services is exactly like selling a promise. You can't prove that you can do it until you have done it! Unlike selling a product which you can take back if it doesn't work, professional services cannot always be undone. You may only get one chance at getting it right or building the house.

So how do you build the trust required so that high value clients choose you ahead of others? This book explains how, based on the assumption that your firm is too broad in its marketing messages, too diverse in its service offering, too unfocused on key areas of expertise and, most importantly, too accepting as just anyone as a client. In other words, **if you want to be a big fish in your pond – rather than making yourself bigger, reduce the size of the pond.**

Paul Watkins

Chapter 1
Three important points

First, a really big POINT

Some years ago I listened to a presentation by the hugely successful New Zealand retail jeweller, Michael Hill. He was addressing an audience of specialist retailers and made a very prophetic comment, "It doesn't matter if you are an expert jeweller, an expert on cell phones or an expert on paint. The only thing that matters is being an expert on filling your shop with customers!"

It's not your professional expertise that fills your diary or your appointment calendar; it's your ability to communicate this (perceived) expertise to your potential clients and develop lasting relationships with them.

Next, a really big WORD

Do you sell any services that are unique to your firm? I would be very surprised if you said 'yes'. Do you offer any of them at lower prices than your competitors? I hope not. Do you work on the (flawed) principle that working more hours will generate more fees?

Whether you are an accountant, financial planner, dentist, tree trimmer, hairdresser, motor vehicle repair garage, pharmacist, lawyer, PR consultant, plumber or IT specialist, the issues are the same – what you are selling cannot be touched, tasted, picked up or sold on E-bay. It's a service, or more correctly, you are selling an idea, a belief, a desired outcome, a pledge or a promise. To put it in a word – **trust**. Prospective clients have to inherently trust you to deliver on that promise to do what you say you can do.

You are swapping time for money and your income is the product of a unit of time and a unit of money. Time is finite, so the only thing you can alter is the dollar value you can place on a unit of your time. This is directly proportional to the perceived value of your offer, or the trust in your ability to deliver on your promise – which in turn is based on perceptions of your expertise in the client's field of interest.

And, now the FISH bit

As the saying goes, it's better to be a big fish in a small pond than a small fish in a big pond. This is the most important principle behind growing a professional services business – which I shall prove to you in the chapters ahead, as well as explaining how to do that.

Chapter 2
Why you MUST aim to be the big fish (in your field)

Who makes more, a GP or a Specialist?

We all know the answer to this, which is the clue to how you become a valuable component of your client's lives. I have a friend who had prostate cancer a few years ago. He panicked a little (as anyone would) and searched the Internet at length to find the "best option in the world". He phoned US, Mexican and Canadian clinics to discuss treatments and then searched for the person considered the "best" in his own country.

Did he get the "best"? He says he did, and whether the surgeon really was the best or not is irrelevant – my friend believed that to be the case and that's all that mattered. Was cost an issue? What do you think?

On matters less life-threatening, when it comes to choosing a doctor for yourself, or a lawyer, an architect, a financial advisor, a plumber or someone to mow your lawns, the most likely first step you would take is to ask around your friends, work colleagues or neighbours. Why? Because quite simply you don't want to take the chance of choosing badly.

This is why advertising for professional services rarely works, which I discuss in another chapter. And if you get a strong recommendation from someone for a specific person, do you question the price or get competitive quotes?

How much are you prepared to pay for the 'best of breed'?

Ever noticed how the 'best of breed' within any category is just so much more expensive than the next best and then the price dramatically falls from there on. Take cars as an example.

The average six cylinder family saloon, costs about US$25,000 (in 2008) and the top of the line version of the same cars, about $35,000. While that's a big jump, the extra $10,000 can sometimes be justified by buyers because of the leather seats, a bigger engine, the built-in GPs, parking sensors, more sound-proofing and so on. But if you want a prestige brand such as BMW, Mercedes or Audi, you will pay over $80,000 for the same full sized car with the same specifications. That's more than three times as much as a standard family salon. And the V12 versions cost an extra $45,000 over and above that! Are they worth that much more? Can you go faster in them (legally)? Do they use less fuel? Cost less to repair? For some reason we are prepared to pay that enormous premium to get the 'best of breed'.

An important point to note is that 'best' in cars is only partly defined as quality, performance and specifications. The real reason we choose to see them as the 'best' is intangible. It's the snobbery factor, the personal satisfaction of feeling of superiority from knowing you can afford such a car. None of these are tangible or truly measurable – yet they can cause us to spend an extra $150,000 to $200,000 on a car.

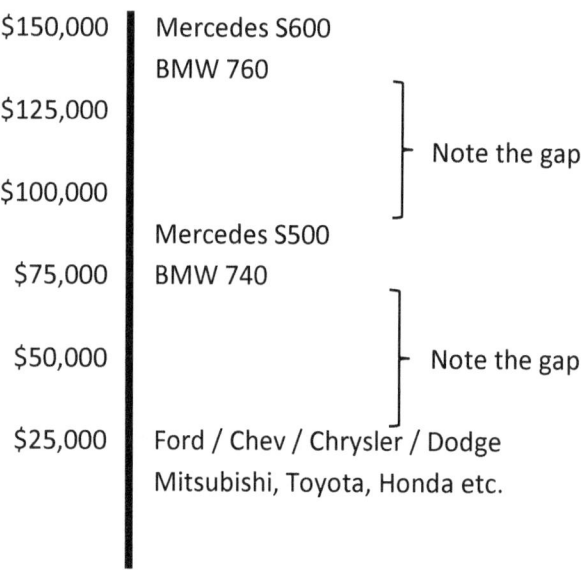

A chart of new car prices of select 4-door saloons in $US in 2008

$150,000	Mercedes S600
	BMW 760
$125,000	
	} Note the gap
$100,000	
	Mercedes S500
$75,000	BMW 740
$50,000	} Note the gap
$25,000	Ford / Chev / Chrysler / Dodge
	Mitsubishi, Toyota, Honda etc.

The lesson here is that if you are 'Number 1' in a segment or niche, you can command an enormous premium – well outside the range of what is considered normal.

You may be wondering how Mercedes and BMW can both be 'number 1' at the same time. In most cases, the brands within a category have been developed with very distinct personas or images. In some cases this is so distinct; it is regarded as a completely different category. Few Mercedes owners would aspire to own a BMW and vice versa. Each one appeals to a different type of buyer. But in both cases, the price difference between ordinary and premium remains.

Let's look at the relative sales of similar products in highly competitive markets

This chart shows the box office receipts for the top 10 movies in the UK for the single weekend of 7-9 December, 2007, in US dollars.

The golden Compass	$14.9 million
Fred Clause	$2.6 million
Hitman	$1.2 million
American Gangster	$550,000
Beowulf	$422,000
Assassination of Jesse James	$246,000
Stardust	$230,000
Ratatouille	$293,000
The Darjeeling Limited	$175,000
Aaja Nachle	$166,000

Note the phenomenal lead of the top earner, which is $12 million ahead of the 2nd place earner at just $2.6 million, which is in turn more than double that of the 3rd biggest draw at $1.2 million. It's like a ski slope from the top to the bottom, ending with 10th place, Aaja Nachle, earning a paltry $166,000

But take a closer look at these figures. Looking at the specific movies, Golden Compass is aimed at a wide audience of both adults and children, whereas The Assassination of Jesse James, earning just $246,000, is squarely and solely aimed at 'thinking adults' wanting a meaty emotion-filled drama.

So, you could successfully argue that The Assassination of Jesse James is 'number 1' in the educated adult market, while the animated kids feature Ratatouille, earning just $293,000, is 'number 1' in the tween/pre-adolescent market that week.

Why you should never be in the middle

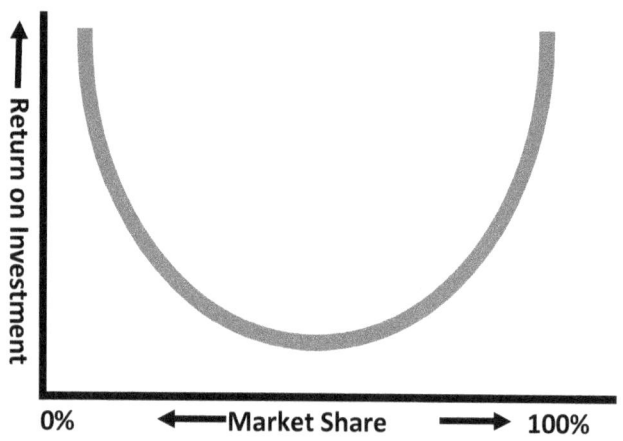

The chart on the previous page represents, in general terms, the return on investment (profit) against market share. Note that if you have total market domination (close to 100%) then you can set your own price and, therefore, your margins can be huge.

Similarly, if you control a niche or market segment, you can command a premium price in exactly the same way. At this end of the chart you have a small market share overall, but this is irrelevant, as your share is huge at a localised or specialist level.

"So your truck was overloaded."

There is a law firm that specialises in helping transport operators when facing traffic violations. Their hourly charge is roughly twice that of other law firms in that city. Why? As a small firm, their overall market share is negligible but in the field of help with heavy transport traffic violations, they reign supreme.

But if you are languishing somewhere in the middle (small fish, big pond) – facing lots of competition with similar offers and have no recognisable competitive edge or specialty, then your prices will be dictated by the market in general and loyalty will be dubious at best as its based no price. This is NOT where you want to be.

So the key to making good money is clearly to either totally dominate the market (big fish, big pond) or find a profitable niche to occupy and dominate (big fish, small pond). The latter is much, much easier to achieve and how to do this is the subject of this book.

What does the bracketed phrase "in your field" in the chapter title mean?

This is the key to becoming the big fish. If you have no obvious point of difference to your intended clients, then pick a niche. Of course you should make sure it's a profitable niche.

Paul Watkins

Chapter 3
The rise and rise and rise of the niche

Words from the master

Seth Godin's quote at the start of the book was:

> "The mass market is dying. There is no longer one best song or one best kind of coffee. Now there are a million micro markets, but each micro market still has a BEST. If your micro market is 'organic markets in Tulsa', then that's your world. And being the best in THAT world is the place to be."

What does this mean? **What is YOUR niche?**

The Long Tail

This is the title of a ground-breaking book by Chris Anderson, (highly recommended reading). It explains how consumer choice has become almost unlimited, primarily due to the Internet, although this has now trickled into all areas of commerce. So the real money is in the 'Long Tail' – the niches. The diagram below is from his book and various web sites, and shows the concept of the Long Tail.

For example, for the music industry, the CD store is disappearing fast. Rather than choosing from the perhaps 800 albums on display in a store, containing to total of 90,000 songs, we can now access any variation of these from more than 1.5
million through Rhapsody.com or iTunes.com.

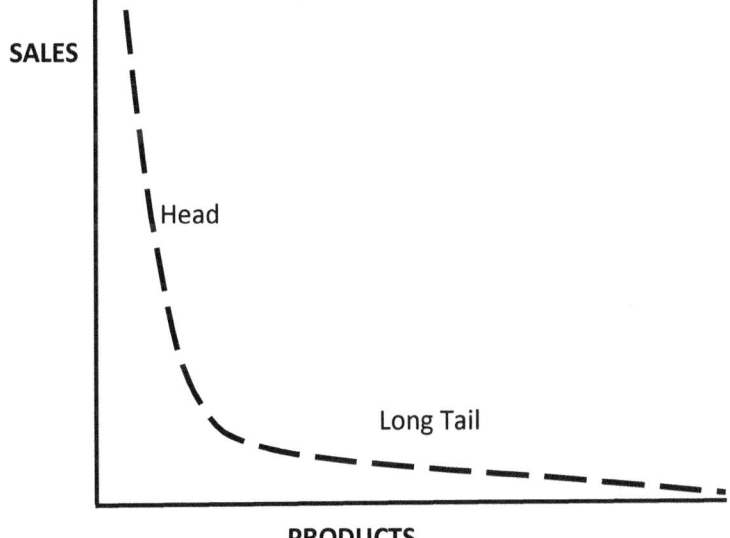

In the past, to make it as a musician you had to be in the top 10 overall. Now, you still have to be in the top handful, but only within your specific niche – which through worldwide market

access via the Internet is entirely feasible. For example, rather than being number one in country music per se (a very big call), you can be number one in 'Southern African-American bluegrass gospel' – and be dominant in that field.

And no, you do not have to have a service that is driven by the Internet for this to work. Your service may not lend itself to the Internet in a product purchase sense, but the principle of the Long Tail (the explosive growth of the niche) certainly applies.

BMW's only please

SD European is a car sales, parts and repair garage in New Zealand that ONLY deals with BMWs. The company has been involved exclusively with the BMW marque since 1984.

It is New Zealand's largest independent BMW specialist and has a very loyal clientele. Why wouldn't they? BMWs are relatively complicated cars compared to your average family saloon and owners are very proud of them, so they want the best in care and attention. SD European also offers loan cars to clients, usually 3-series BMWs.

Can a firm exist only servicing a single marquee of car? And a luxury brand at that? There is a wait of up to a week to get your car in, which is a clear sign of the popularity of, and loyalty to, the service.

A TV channel for food lovers

Decades ago there was one TV channel in New Zealand, and then we got a couple more. But now there are hundreds of TV channels and more being added at regular intervals.

Notice however, that each new one is extremely specific in its target audience and programme offering. There is one specifically for food lovers, one for history buffs, and one that offers only cartoons. Each one has a highly defined loyal audience. So while the overall viewer share of the cartoon channel is negligible, it is probably number one for four to nine year olds.

The death of the 'one-size-fits-all' offer

Chris Anderson proposes that market niches that were not viable just a few years ago are now very profitable, as this phenomenon of The Long Tail has effectively killed the market for any 'one-size-fits-all' product or service. Consumers now want the version specifically designed for them or designed to do a highly specific task. So if you have "One Stop Shop" written anywhere in you advertising – delete it. It is not what clients want.

"No extra charge for the fax."

Does it annoy you when you check out of your hotel to find a list of tiny extras on the bill? They might be listed as optional extras, but to you as the business traveller they are essential parts of any stay so you expect them to be included.

US-based Wingate Inns exclusively targets the business traveler looking for mid-priced accommodation. Realising that it's the little things that annoy their chosen market, all necessary options such as Internet access, fax, copying, printing, local phone calls, spa pool, fitness centre and breakfast are all included in the package.

Does it work? By focusing on this single target market, Wingate was chosen as the top mid-range hotel by Wall Street's Smart Money magazine, and Bill Gates nominated them for a Computerworld Smithsonian Award for business travel services.

By being single-minded about their target market, they now operate more than 250 hotels throughout the US, Canada, East and West Europe and the Middle East.

"Bloatware" or "Feature creep"

Bloatware. *(blōt´wãr) (n.) jargon. Software that has lots of not necessarily useful features and requires considerable disk space and RAM.*

As the cost of RAM and disk storage has decreased, there has been a growing trend among software developers to disregard the size of applications. An example is printer upgrade software that can be hundreds of megabytes in size, just to fix a small glitch and add one little-used feature.

Some people refer to this trend as 'Feature Creep'. This is when the developer gets carries away with their own prowess and keeps adding cute features and nice visual effects that will have dubious or no real application. They are misguided into thinking it will impress the consumer and make their software more attractive.

Bloatware and Feature Creep have made it into our business vocabulary in recent years, not only in respect of software, but also to describe the myriad of products and services that have tried to appeal to too many markets at the same time and missed them all by doing so. This is a very easy trap to fall into as the next section reveals.

Feature Creep is alive and well in professional services

Pick any section in the Yellow Pages. Advertisements frequently feature apparently unrelated lists of bullet points. Lawyers list every key aspect of law, plumbers list at least eight separate and specific types of work they can do for you.

The problem here is that you end up looking confused and not at all like an expert in any of the fields you list. If you have three distinct target markets, then you are better to have three separate smaller advertisements, each one specific to the market concerned.

Depth of range is a fallacy

Feature Creep doesn't work! Retailers regularly fall into this trap. An example would be a pharmacy that offers nine different cold remedies, 16 different antihistamines, seven ways to cure head lice and four foot odour cures. The public are easily confused and out of the 16 antihistamines, would probably only recognise the two market leading brands.

You don't go to a pharmacy for a range to choose from. You go for the 'best' remedy for your current condition. You rely on the pharmacy staff to decide for you which one is appropriate based on their expert knowledge and experience.

Social psychologists, Professor Sheena Iyengar, PhD from Columbia University Business School, and Mark Lepper, PhD, a psychology professor at Stanford University, were the first to demonstrate the downside of excessive choice. In their famous JAM experiment, the results were surprising.

There were just too many jams!

Iyengar and Lepper's first field experiment was in basic consumer choice. While out grocery shopping, consumers encountered a tasting booth which displayed either a limited (6), or an extensive (24) selection of different flavours of jam. The aim was to examine whether the number of options on offer affected consumer's subsequent purchasing behaviour.

Consumers were allowed to taste as many jams as they wished. All consumers who approached the table received a coupon allowing them one dollar off any purchase of the jam.

The results: Nearly 30% of the consumers in the limited-choice condition subsequently purchased a jar of jam. By contrast, only 3% of the consumers in the extensive-choice condition purchased a jar of jam. Thus, consumers initially exposed to limited-choices proved considerably more likely to purchase the product than consumers who had initially encountered a much larger set of options.

This study was reinforced by psychologist Alexander Chernev, PhD, of Northwestern University. Chernev found that when people were offered variants of the same brand of toothpaste, e.g. cavity prevention, tartar-control and teeth-whitening types, they tended to switch to another brand that offered a single option.

But professional services is NOT jam!

Sheena Iyengar also sought to examine consumer choices with higher stakes by analysing retirement fund choices. These ranged from packages of two options to 59 choices and to validate the survey, the test sample was huge – 800,000 employees at 647 companies.

The results: "Instead of leading to more thoughtful choosing, more options led people to act like the jam buyers", says Iyengar. "When given two choices, 75% participated in the schemes, but when given 59 choices, only 60% did." In addition, she found that the greater the number of options, the more cautious people were with their investment strategies.

Also found was that "Too much choice can lead people to make simple snap judgments just to avoid the hassle of wading through confusing options." This ironically can sabotage a company's marketing plan if they wish to be seen as the expert in that field.

Chapter 4
If you don't find a niche you won't be able to grow

How come your growth flattened out?

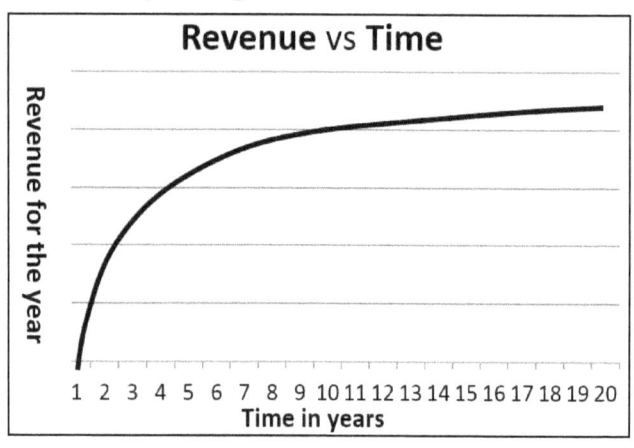

In the early days of your professional services career did you see substantial growth each year and then it started to flatten out? Many find that after year five, growth is very small and in many cases only in line with inflation. The graph above is typical of the growth curve for many. Why does the growth flatten out? It is not because you have filled up all the hours, but because of where your business is coming from and how you are spending your time. The graph on the previous page can be applied to almost all firms selling time.

Graph clients vs cumulative business

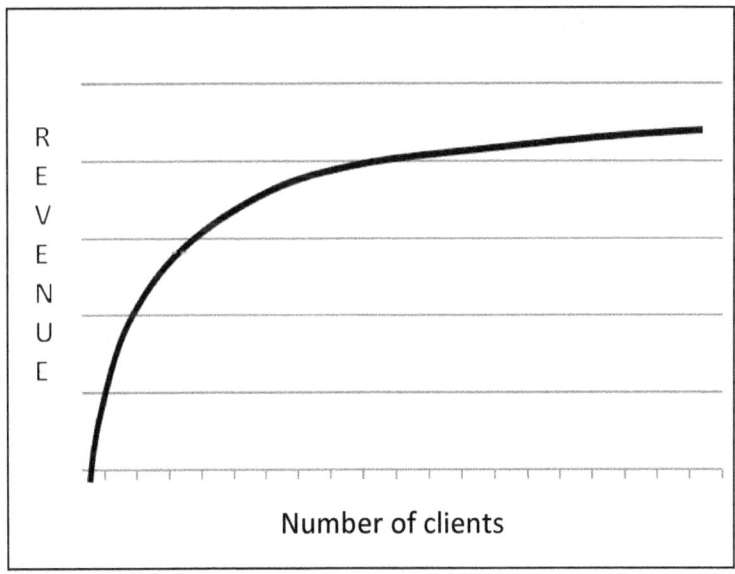

The obvious thing about this graph is the match in the curve to the previous graph.

The Pareto Principle says that 80% of your business will come from 20% of your customers. It is extremely rare to find a business in any industry where this isn't true. With easy to use clientbase management tools now available, you can segment your clients into categories based on their value to your business. How do you do this? This is a frequently asked question, so I will answer it based on the example in the graph. If this were my clientbase, I would categorise it like this:

- The top 15 clients are worth 25% of the revenue and would therefore become 'A' clients
- The next 155 are 'B' clients. (A+B are 80% of revenue)
- The rest are 'C' clients

This segmentation allows for the development of a simple, cost-effective client contact strategy, allocating time and resources where they should be to grow the firm. The strategies for the three segments can be summarised as:

- **A-clients**: love them dead, with a view to replicating them. These are the ones that make the real money for the firm.
- **B-clients**: a high level of pre-programmed personal service to each, being the responsibility of an allocated staff member. These clients keep the firm alive.
- **C-clients**: Sell them, give them to others, delete them, above all do nothing to encourage them to send their friends. You do NOT want more of them.

Now consider the two case studies on the next two pages.

They thought they had 5,500 clients, but then they looked a little closer.

A legal firm had 5,500 clients. Upon going through the firm's records, we discovered that (in round figures):

- 3,400 hadn't been seen in the last 5 years, in part because 700 of them had DIED!
- 2,000 of these hadn't been seen for 10 years or more
- They didn't <u>want</u> to see 400 ever again!
- Of those seen inside the past 5 years, over 1,000 were just for small conveyancing jobs or basic wills.
- Only 600 had been seen in the past 12 months, of which less than 100 were considered active high value clients.

This active 600 represented just 11% of the total number of clients. Following a most revealing profitability analysis, they found that the **600 (11%) active clients** accounted for **90% of the firm's profit** and the **top 100** for **half of the profit.** This is because the work is focused, ongoing, never discounted and in often based around a monthly retainer. How they changed their firm and significantly increased their profitability overall is told in Chapter 14.

Less overheads, less stress, more family time, more money...

Sounds like the ideal job! Well it happened to a partner in a large accountancy practice. He had responsibility for 107 clients of the firm. He had a small team around him and the constant pressure of the 107 all wanting help. He typically worked 60+ hours a week.

He knew there had to be a better way, particularly as the time he was able to devote to his family was suffering badly. So he analysed his revenue and discovered that just three clients generated the bulk of the fees (surprise, surprise).

After coming to an arrangement with his partners, he left the firm and worked solely for his three key clients. He worked out of their respective offices (so didn't need his own office) for one full day a week for each.

He now works just three days a week, which his family appreciates) and has little work related stress. And the clients love it. But a really interesting outcome is that with no overheads his personal income has gone up considerably as he still charges the same hourly rate!

Paul Watkins

Chapter 5
Who do you really, really want as clients?

Do some clients annoy you?

Some are a real pain in the rear and cause stress and anxiety as soon as they call. So, the obvious question is why do you deal with them? There is no law to say that you have to. It's entirely your choice who you deal with

On the other side of the coin, there are clients that are an absolute joy to work with. The type of work you do for them is challenging and rewarding. They are appreciative of your efforts and never question your invoices. Imagine if all your clients were like that. So why can't they be?

Two questions to ask prospective clients

Personally, I screen my prospects using two questions when they first enquire about using my services. Sometimes I ask the questions either just as they are written below and at other times I learn the answers more subtly during the conversation. Either way I end up knowing the answers.

The first question is: "Can you afford me?" I do not want to get into debates about travel costs or wanting discounted rates because they can't really afford it. If you get a hint of this right up front, find a way to recommend someone else.

The second question is: "Do I like you?" which can also be asked as, "Are you and I going to be able to work together in an atmosphere of mutual respect?" What I want to know is whether it is going to be a pleasurable experience dealing with them or are they going to constantly question any advice I offer or be closed minded to new ideas. This advice might sound a touch arrogant, but your business life will become so much more enjoyable and lucrative once you follow it.

Reactive versus proactive

Most professional service providers simply wait for the phone to ring. They are REACTIVE marketers rather than being PROACTIVE.

In my experience few believe that they can be anything else. Most think it's too hard to advertise to attract specific client types and since they have to bill at least 75% of a typical day, a few bad ones among the good is okay. If you cling to these principles then you can't possibly grow.

How to be a big fish

Pick your favourites

		Simon Smith	Mary Marne	Kevin Strong	John Possum	Marie Stewart	Steve Green	Scott Wilson	Name
		CFO	Mid Mgr	Self Emp	Owner	CFO	CFO	Owner	Occupation or title
		Timber Coy	Engineer	Prop Develop	Painter	Car dealer	Fishing	Building	Industry
		Type 1	Type 1	Type 3	Type 1	Type 1	Type 2	Type 1	Type of work done
		LRR	TB	Y/Pg	MG	MG	GB	MG	How they became a client
		45	40	55	50	45	40	51	Age (best guess)
		M	F	M	M	F	M	M	Gender
		Cars	Travel	Flying	Fishing	??	Boats	Yachts	Interests

The first step in getting ready to put a growth strategy in place is to pick your favourites. You do this by going through your client base and picking out your best/favourite 20 clients. You can make this your top 10, 15 or top 25 if you wish, depending on what type of service you offer, but don't go beyond 25.

Don't pick these just based on value. They key here is that they should be the ones you would most like to replicate. You may have a particular area of expertise you enjoy working in, a particular type of job that allows your creativity to shine, or a type of customer who you know you can truly add value to or appreciates your knowledge.

Now put them into a chart like the example on the previous page. Include as many columns as you like to describe key characteristics, the more the better. Make sure they include personal characteristics as these can often give a clue as to why you seem to get on better with some more than others.

There is no doubt at all that a pattern will emerge. The first time I did this myself, I found that 13 of my best 20 clients were females aged in their 30s who held a specific type of role in the firms I spoke/consulted to. I also found that two professions dominated my top 20. While I had sort of been aware of this, it was quite a surprise to see just how important they were.

Recording the personal details also lets you know who best to direct your marketing activity at. Most of the time it will not be the CEO, and a curious fact is that most of your best clients will be within seven years either side of your own age.

There is no such thing as business to business marketing (B2B)

To reinforce the value of doing this exercise, there is an important issue that we should discuss. 'B2B' is a trendy term that gets thrown around by executives to describe the fact that their customers are other firms or business entities. WRONG!!!

If you think this then your marketing will be based on flawed logic. A firm or business entity is a piece of paper in a file in a lawyer's office. It cannot trade. It is a piece of paper. It is very important to understand that. **PEOPLE DEAL WITH PEOPLE**.

No matter how 'logical' the fit of the service or product, it will always come back to TRUST. Do you TRUST that the person can deliver on the promise that they are making to you? You will of course have heard things said like, "the deal was done on the golf course", or "The real business at the conference was concluded in the bar after the formal sessions".

Or, "I made an incredible contact in the coffee break at the seminar". These are not just chance events, they are repeating. You must get to know who you are dealing with and appeal to them as people, not just the firm they represent.

Appeal to the person, not the firm – it's all about people!

This case study comes from the pages of international best-selling book 'Guerrilla Marketing'.

An investment bank decided to try to sell services to the 100 largest companies in America. A rather big ask you might say.

Their target was the CFO in each corporation, who until then had not been interested in talking to them. So they rethought their approach and looked to the person, rather than the strength of the offer.

They sent the CFOs a baseball each week for three weeks, each baseball autographed by a famous player. They also sent a 4-place display stand with the first one. Instead of a fourth baseball, they sent a note saying that it would be hand delivered by their account manager at a time that allowed for a short presentation on what the bank could offer their organisation. Not wanting to miss out on the ball, 80% of the CFOs set up an appointment with the bank's account manager!

The baseballs cost US$200 each and the display stand $50, meaning $850 per prospect. But it reportedly led to over $100 million in business.

Let's go back to why you are doing the chart of best clients

The whole point of this exercise is to identify who you would like to replicate. If you could add 20 more clients to your clientbase, who would you like them to be? More bottom end 'C' clients? I doubt it. As they say, "Never ask a 'C' client for a referral, because you will get another 'C; client!

By identifying specifically who you want more of, you can be much more targeted in your marketing activities. It may be that you have seven out of the twenty in the IT industry or perhaps five in the medical profession. This will give a clue as to where your prospecting efforts should be directed as you know you can offer valued expertise to these professions.

Perhaps the pattern that emerges is the type of work you like doing. You realise that the clients you want to replicate are all ones you offer knowledge X to. Looking through the hypothetical chart a few pages earlier, since referrals from 'MG' appears as the reason you gained three of your top clients, you should have a special plan for maintaining and developing that relationship, so that MG continues to give referrals.

In my case, as I said above, I discovered a high number of people with very similar titles or responsibilities within their firms (which would account in part for their gender and closeness in age). So from that point on, when I approached a firm to offer my services, I ensured that the person carrying that title was present. It saves time and leads to more favourable outcomes.

Paul Watkins

Chapter 6
How to become the big fish in your chosen field

Procrustean Strategies

In Greek mythology, Procrustes was a bandit from Attica. He had a hotel in the hills outside Eleusis. There, he invited every passerby to stay in the one bed that he had. If the guest proved too tall, he would amputate the excess length; if the victim was found too short, he was then stretched on the bed until he fit. Of course the guests died from these 'body adjustments' and Procrustes kept their belongings.

A very common way to offer services is to make the offer based on a generic one-size-fits-all offer regardless of what the market wants. For example – "We service all makes of car" or "Builders of beautiful homes" or "No section too big or too small – we mow them all". Such strategies have become known as 'Procrustean Strategies' for obvious reasons – and prove to be just as unsuccessful. Find the market first then frame your offer to fit the target market, not the other way around.

Porter's three Competitive Strategies

In 1980, Michael Porter, a professor at Harvard Business School, wrote a book called 'Competitive Strategy'. In it he proposed that there are only three ways you can have a sustainable competitive edge:

1. **Price** leadership (in your chosen market)
2. **Differentiation** based on a key attribute
3. **Focus** on a market segment or service offer

There is no fourth option. The next three chapters cover each of these in turn.

'There can be only one'

This is the title of theme song by Queen for the movie Highlander, which perfectly describes the fact that there you can choose only one thing to be the best at. This is an advertisement I recently found:

> As a specialist in new home building, renovations and light commercial, we offer the highest quality construction at surprisingly low prices

Yeah right! Which one are they trying to be? Are they focusing on being a specialist in a type of construction (in which category?) or are they saying that they are the price leaders or are they using the differentiator of quality building?

You can only have one because they are incompatible. How can the highest quality be at the lowest price? That's like saying 'BMW 7-series now at lower prices than any other cars on the market'. Similarly, a Cardiologist that says he is a specialist in cancer as well as gynaecological and endocrinology services would not have many rush to make an appointment for any of those medical issues.

Be clear in what you want to be known for. For example, let's say you put yourself forward as a specialist in renovations for the property investor. Clients will expect to pay more for your services. But since you are the specialist in that field, they will be comfortable that you know how to minimise the time and cost on their behalf – and are very unlikely to seek competitive quotes. Similarly, if you offer "affordable" building services, the sort of clients you attract (just wanting a cheap job) will never expect you to win the award for the 'Quality Home of the Year'. Which one you choose as your specialty is entirely dependent on who you want to attract as clients.

Paul Watkins

Chapter 7
Using PRICE as a strategy

Being the price leader

Examples of price leadership are particularly apparent in retail. New Zealand retail giant, The Warehouse, sells itself on the idea that 'everyone gets a bargain' and offers the everyday living product range at a price ending in 99 cents to reinforce this. Quality is dubious at times, but that doesn't matter as they offer a no-questions 100% money back or replacement guarantee.

In every market there will be a price leader – someone that has a deliberate strategy of undercutting the others. They may not say 'cheapest' or 'lowest price', but be a little more subtle, using terms like 'affordable' and 'why pay more than you should?' This is a very difficult position to maintain as in every market there is someone who will underprice you just to get the work on the pretext of a foot in the door, or generating cashflow or some other illogical reason.

Less reputable real estate agents use this technique in reverse. It is called 'buying the listing', whereby they deliberately tell the vendor they can sell the house for a price that they know to be unrealistically high. The vendor then gives them sole agency and a week or two later they return to say 'the market says you should lower your price' – to the value they knew to be correct when they first gained the listing.

There should be very few circumstances or markets (unless you offer a pure off-the-shelf commodity) where you would use a low price offer as your competitive advantage. Read the following sections before contemplating this.

The $5 milkshake

Sometimes raising your price to well above those of your competition can work in your favour. It creates desire, anticipation, perceived quality and snob value.

In the movie Pulp Fiction, John Travolta is sitting in the restaurant with Uma Thurman and she orders a milkshake that costs $5. (Assume a normal price of less than $1). Travolta is stunned that a shake can cost that much and says "I gotta know what a $5 shake tastes like". He sips it and then proclaims, "It's a pretty f***ing good milkshake". Is it five times as good as a normal one? Of course not, but his anticipation of one costing that much and tasting better is such that it must be.

Give this idea some consideration before setting your pricing structure – but make sure that it is part of an overall plan, notably involving a clear brand strategy. An example is the elite positions the BMW 760 and the Mercedes S600 occupy (see Chapter 3). They cost little more to make than the slightly smaller engined BMW 750 and

S500, yet are deliberately priced $50,000 higher to generate the desire and undoubted snobbery factor.

Rolex is another example of a very high priced item that does not perform any better than others in its category, yet maintains its legendary status almost entirely as the result of the huge price it carries. Perrier water is another example. Water is water, yet Perrier is somehow "better". Surely it must be, it costs so much more than the others.

Fixed price service

A successful variation is offering fixed prices or something like "we quote before starting and stick to the quote regardless of what we find". Here, there is no reference to whether you are high or low priced in your service, but a lot of research concludes that people want to know what they are up for before the work starts. Not knowing what the bill will be beforehand can be stressful.

Many professional service providers are reluctant to offer quotes, preferring to offer an estimate or a range that the cost will likely fall within. Particularly with lawyers and accountants; this is because quoting in advance challenges their internal charging system of six minute units. Just because it suits you to charge that way, it rarely suits the client – the one that pays.

Real estate firms that offer fixed fee commission structures regardless of the value of the property have been popping up. This approach appeals to many clients. Similarly, fixed cost auto repair shops, fixed cost dentistry and fixed cost accounting services are emerging. It is an approach worth considering.

Paul Watkins

Chapter 8
Using a point of DIFFERENTIATION

How are you slightly different?

A plumber uses the slogan: "We can be there in 60 minutes". And a pizza delivery service uses, "Pizzas to you in 45 minutes or you don't pay". These are both examples of finding a point of differentiation (in this case speed of delivery of service).

A point of differentiation can be based on a customer service attribute such as the enormously successful line from Avis, "We try harder". Or a mortgage broker who says, "I can meet you at the open home on Sunday – just call"   It can be based on a specific attribute such as a car repair garage that uses, "Loan cars available for EVERY customer", or a butcher who advertises "Free parking right outside our door".

Once identified, this point can lead to your tag line or slogan, although don't be hung up on that. Using it in headlines, in references in articles and reinforcing it in newsletter articles is the way to make it work for you. If it can be worked into a short tag line, that's even better but I find that many firms get very hung up on tag lines and miss the point of the exercise.

Make sure it implies that your competitors do the opposite

This is the key to using a point of differentiation to distinguish yourself from your competitors. When Coca Cola used 'The real thing', it implied that Pepsi, RC and other colas were me-too pretenders. When Hertz said 'We are number 1', Avis responded with 'We try harder' which implied that big is not necessarily best. The loan car offer from the repair shop implies that others don't – which customers know.

What is your point of difference?

To work out if you have a genuine point of difference, use a chart like the one below. Put you and your 4 main competitors along the top and list key attributes of your service offer down the side. When you find a line where the only tick is in your column then you may be onto something.

In this example of an auto repair service, on the face of it there are few areas of differentiation. But the fact that they offer loan cars

	You	1	2	3	4
Long opening hours		√		√	
Clean car for you		√	√	√	
Loan car	√				
Free pick up/delivery	√	√	√	√	√
Technical equipment		√	√		
Experience of team	√		√		
Specialise in BMWs	√	√			
Located in city centre		√			√

to every customer that needs one is a huge benefit and one that others don't offer. The specialisation in BMWs and experience of the team are important, but the free pickup and delivery is clearly a universal offering.

And a quick comment before you do this – it could well be a small thing, like the parking outside the butcher shop, or the mortgage broker offering to work on a Sunday. You could ask your next 20 clients why they chose you as an indication of what seems to make a difference. The examples listed previously are for a fictitious car repair garage.

"We pride ourselves on our service"

"Service" has to be the most clichéd, overused and abused word in business today. It's made worse by nonsensical slogans such as 'Service is our middle name' and 'Our service is our difference'. And what must be the worst of all, 'Service with attitude'. These are all meaningless drivel and completely useless in terms of driving sales, but service can be used as a competitive advantage if it is understood.

If you genuinely believe that service is your edge, there are a few things to consider. First, "good service" is a worthless phrase as no one would say that they provide bad service, so what are you really saying? To make it mean something, it must be specific. It should be said in terms of speed of delivery, concierge parking, daily updates on progress, you travel to them, loan cars available and so on. Be very specific about the aspect of good service that you know impresses clients.

And service is a relative term, but relative to what the client expects, not your competitors. If clients expect 48 hour turnaround, then if you can do it in 24 hours, you are considered to offer brilliant service on that point. However, if you perform the service in the expected 48 hours, clients see you as average.

Be very conscious of exactly what it is that constitutes good service. Expectations are rising, so what was fine ten years ago is no longer good enough now. In retail, not being open at the weekends is frowned upon by customers and law offices that close for a month over Christmas are aften criticised. Understanding your client's needs and meeting or exceeding them is the way to be considered as offering good service.

'Good service' is NOT an edge

Why don't you tip every waiter? Many research studies show that restaurant guests do NOT tip for efficient speedy service. Incredibly they tip slow and inefficient service just as well.

Instead, we tip when they are made to feel special. Smiles, a joke, a little touch, pleasant conversation and taking what appears to be a genuine interest in the customer earn much higher tips than having the food delivered on time. A standout reason for tipping was discovered to be remembering the customer from a previous visit.

So what are the lessons here? Things like delivering on time, and not keeping clients waiting are not 'good service', they are fundamental good manners. But asking how a client's new car is, because you remembered that they were buying one from last time, can constitute service that deserves a tip. Give your professional service with a personality.

Paul Watkins

Chapter 9
Using FOCUS as a strategy

Choosing a focus

A focus can be on a geographical area (e.g. like real estate agents), a specific service (e.g. being a guru on IT networks for hospitals), a specific market segment (e.g. BMW drivers), a type of client (e.g. retired people only) or a single industry (e.g. financial services). It can even be a combination of two or more (e.g. an expert on existing client base marketing for insurance agents). There are no rules. The point being to become an expert in your chosen field or to your chosen segment.

If you really want to grow your business, this is the biggie in terms of bang-for-buck. This is the easiest to implement and usually the most successful of the strategies. This is because it leads to you being the big fish by reducing the size of the pond.

Become world famous in one city block

A geographical focus can be extremely successful. To explain this, most retailers get 80% of their business from within a three kilometre radius of their front door. So, why would they advertise on the radio when it reaches the entire city population when 80% of the customers are so close. Mass advertising may work for a retail chain of course with multiple locations.

Geographically the area can literally be one city block, as an insurance broker found out. In his case he was located within an industrial estate and he could almost see all of his large clients from his front door. So he started a "Protecting our Estate" newsletter to the businesses around him, which included little pieces of news about the estate itself: local authority planning issues that may be of interest, new tenant profiles, a directory to encourage businesses in the area to use each other, and, of course, regular articles on business and personal insurance. It was hand delivered by one of his staff to increase the relationship opportunity. Did it work? Yes!

You can have more than one at once

I am considered to have industry specific marketing expertise by both the financial services sector and retail pharmacies – two apparently completely different styles of business. (Actually there are huge similarities in how they offer and market their services, as both are advice-based businesses). I can focus on them both, as they are clearly not in competition with each other – or even need to know that I work for the other.

You don't have to think that you are limiting your business by focusing on single a specific area. But don't get carried away. You cannot be an 'expert' to 10 segments. It would be impossible for you to find the time to genuinely learn what you had to know about each one. Just pick two or three.

A vet who put dots on a map

A city vet practice was using radio and press to attract new customers, but was not convinced that it was working. So he put dots on a map to mark the addresses of his customers (since he kept a database). He was surprised to learn that over 70% came from a single suburb and a further 20% from a neighbouring suburb up a valley.

So he stopped his media advertising and started a letterbox dropped newsletter that was seasonal in its topics. For example the main headline read, "What to do with your pets while you are on your summer holiday", "Issues cats face over winter" and "Critical considerations if your dog is alone during the day". He also arranged to write a regular column in the local free newspaper. Customer numbers increased and existing customers used his services more often.

He also kept an eye on the neighbouring suburb identified in the dots-on-a-map exercise and eventually opened a second surgery there, which became a success as well, using the same marketing techniques.

Financial advisors who focus with pinpoint accuracy

A life insurance advisor targets IT professionals and has a large chunk of clients in that industry. Another one has done very well targeting the medical profession.

A fire and general insurance firm targets the members of trade associations by offering policies that suit the peculiarities of the members businesses and with the bonus of bulk rates on the basis of the number of members (although the discount is not huge). These individual members are offered the deal through their own association's mailers and reps, promoted as a member benefit, so much of the sales effort is done for him. So it's a win-win for all parties and the insurance advisory firm has now picked up a few more national associations because of the reputation they have built up working with the first one.

A life insurance advisor, specialising in business insurance, has taken this one step further and specialises in manufacturers owned by partnerships. Another has chosen UK immigrants as the niche and sorts out the transfer of their UK pensions.

One life insurance advisor has found a successful (very high value) niche with farming clients, while one general insurance brokerage focuses on classic and vintage cars and another on light aircraft.

Many more examples exist, all of which have proved to be successful for the business proprietors concerned.

"But how can I focus on a particular market, when that means dealing with competing clients within that market?"

An excellent question. The easiest way around this is to pick a market segment where this doesn't matter. Examples would include: business travellers, BMW drivers, lifestyle block owners and people five years away from retirement. None of these people would care if their competitor or neighbour also uses your services, they just want their own needs met.

"I'm sorry, that's outside my field of expertise, but I have a colleague…"

A lawyer who helps set up a trust for you may then say "I can also do the trademarking for your new business, and the sale and purchase of your new house and also represent you in court over your traffic violation." So he's an expert in what? Nothing from what I can gather.

Its easy to think that you are impressing a client by offering a one-stop shop, making it easy for them. But the issue is that YOU are the one offering to do it all. You are saying 'I am a Jack of all trades and Master of none.' To put it another way – you cannot possibly be an expert in everything for the same clients. Going one step further – if you try, your credibility can fade dramatically.

Professional services are full of generalists. A large number know enough about everything to get by – certainly more than the clients anyway. But it's very easy to think that you may miss the sale or that you know enough to get by and keep the client happy. BAD MISTAKE! Not only do you run the risk of facing a loss of faith from the client, but you can build far more credibility if you say "I'm sorry that's outside my field of expertise, but I have a colleague that can help you with that."

Why does this work better than doing it all yourself? There are two key reasons. First, it confirms your expertise in your own nominated field. By saying, "that's not my field of expertise" you are defining your own field of expertise – the thing that the client will remember you for and not question your fees for. You must be famous for something and "all services in your profession" is not that something.

Second, collaborating with other professionals may lead to referrals. This is an opportunity to form alliances with those in complimentary services that you refer clients to. And, by the way, don't be afraid to use the words "expert" or "guru" or similar. If you say it often enough the people start believing it. This issue was illustrated to me in my early days as a speaker. I was being interviewed for keynote speech at a convention and the interviewer asked how I could add value to the audience. I mentioned a range of marketing topics hoping that one of them would cause a spark of interest.

But then he asked, "Yeah, that's all fine but what are you really passionate about?" It hit me that I had fallen into the same trap that I am discussing here. I was generalising to get the business, which didn't have a hope of working. So I said, "The only thing that really matters in business is making sure you sit in front of the right clients and build solid long-term mutually profitable relationships. I can tell your delegates how to do that". Nothing more was said, I got the booking.

Invent your own category

Al Ries and Jack Trout, in their book 'The 22 Immutable Laws of Marketing' ask who the first person was to fly the Atlantic. Charles Lindberg of course. A name few would not have heard of. But who was second? What about third? Interestingly, you will have heard of the third person – Amelia Earhart. This is not because she was the third person, but because she was the first woman!

In the late 1980s, a few insurance advisers who were inclined to look more holistically at their client's financial lives, came up with the idea of calling themselves 'financial planners'. Rather than focusing on just life insurance, they first consider the longer term financial goals of the client and then align the debt, insurance, investment, budget and legal strategies with these. This has been hugely successful and many charge healthy fees, as well as earn various forms of commission on the products.

As well as looking wider as the financial planners did, consider if there are specific aspects of your service that can be spun off to form their own specific category. Examples in the motor trade are auto-electricians, brake specialists, transmission services, muffler replacement and tyres. At some stage in history they would have all been lumped within the category of 'motor vehicle repair' but as expertise has increased, so have the spin off trades.

Already dominating a high value niche within months of opening

ChanceryGreen is a New Zealand legal practice specialising in environmental law. This covers a range of legal work that includes high end infrastructure, energy, development and climate change work.

The firm was set up in 2007, by three partners from a firm that saw the need for a specialist environmental law practice, not one that just had an environmental law department. So ChanceryGreen was born.

The name choice was important as it had to reflect the style of law and sound modern, exciting and fresh. The decision not to use their surnames was a no brainer, since they are Price, Welsh and Sly. The name plays on the green theme, which is carried through into colours and use of 100% recycled and chlorine free paper. The use of the name Chancery goes beyond their location in the Chancery development of Auckland, as it is also name for the Courts of Equity in England.

Becoming an instant success, the firm now employs three partners, three senior associates, five lawyers and support staff – after just six months of trading.

Interestingly, they quickly discovered that the market wanted to be serviced by the individual partners, not the firm they used to be a part of. (More proof that professional services is ALWAYS based on relationships and not firms) The New Zealand pond for good environment lawyers is not a particularly large one and clients soon tracked the three partners down.

Something that irks many clients is to get a token input from the partner, with most work performed by one of the 'minnows' in the firm. ChanceryGreen has a clear organisational goal of avoiding this model and having high partner involvement. The downside of this is that it requires keeping large and complex work streams, to sustain the higher partner involvement. However, work came in almost immediately from previous clients and referrals. Marketing consists of one of the partners speaking at relevant conferences of potential clients and interaction with other professional firms who have a connection to their target market.

They also walk the talk. They focus on becoming carbon neutral; important, given a number of their clients are going through the process as well.

In the context of the legal profession, while they are hardly a big fish in terms of law firm size, for an environment practice they are already comparable with the national environment teams within full service firms. As one of only two boutique environment firms nationally, they are already the larger.

Paul Watkins

Chapter 10
Do you have a brand or just a name?

"We always buy XX peanut butter, because it tastes so much better"

A tester placed three jars of peanut butter in front of a number of consumers. In blind tests, where the tasters couldn't see the brand names, tasters chose Brand X nearly 80% of the time – because it tasted better.   But in tests that were not blind – that is, where tasters saw the brand names – they picked Brand Y. In fact, tasters chose Brand Y 70% of the time because they recognised that brand more than the other two.

Brand recognition, brand association and brand comfort are all terms that describe this phenomenon. People buy brands or have strong images of brands in their minds. This is the mind-boggling power of branding. (This test is from the book 'Marketing Myths That Are Killing Businesses,' by Kevin Clancy and Robert Shulman).

Is your brand good enough?

Do your teenage kids accept the idea of wearing $29.95 bulk store sneakers or do they only wear $300 Nike sunners? Brands work! You can trade under whatever brand you like so long as you follow some 'rules' of branding. This chapter explains how.

> **"If you want to sell to your least valuable customers, what you are going to brand is your product. If you want to sell to your most valuable customers, you are going to brand the relationship"** - *Martha Rogers PhD*

First, consider NOT changing your brand

Before you launch into a possible brand change, look closely at how you are using your current brand. Branding in professional services is primarily achieved at the individual relationship level anyway. So it may be a case of just simplifying your brand. For example, don't call yourself "H K Smith Professional Services". Either drop the HK or spell your name out, i.e. 'Smith Professional Services' or 'Horace Smith Professional Services'. Initials are hard to remember.

While qualifiers or descriptors can sometimes be a good idea, don't fill it up with clumsy or too many qualifiers, for example, 'Mary Smith Insurance, Investments and Mortgages'. If you use some, keep them very short.

"It's the first letters of all our names"

Sometimes this sort of name can work, but not very often. Nike, Xerox and Pepsi are all made up names, as are Lexus, Compaq and Laser. Most drug names are made up as derivatives of the core ingredient they contain. The downside of this approach is that they are hard to remember until they are established, which can take a lot longer when using this sort of name.

Another issue with this approach is that it can be mis-spelled too often. Consider parents that name their kids Chynna, Shailyn, Jayda, Qualin, Leighanne or Tirrel. (These are all real registered names). Searching for them in the online Yellow Pages or Google would be incredibly difficult.

My name's spelled 'Luxury Yacht' but it's pronounced Throatwobbler Mangrove

This is a line from a famous Monty Python skit. Whatever your brand, it must be easy to pronounce. Here are some more real people's names – how on earth do you pronounce them? Chelyndra, Cyann, Kryzlyannie and Shiarian.

CBE, ADW, IBT, CNW, CNN, CUA, UPS

These are all real firms that with a few exceptions have no brand presence at all. The ones that have are because of their time in business, size and media presence. Many started off using their full name and common usage shortened it.

It is an error to use your initials only, such as 'MSPS' for Mary Smith Professional Services. No one can remember them, they are virtually unsearchable and they do nothing for your brand image. Unless you find that your clients already use them as a shortened version of your current name, then forget it.

It's all about ME!

Using your own name or that of your founder can be successful, for example, Michael Hill Jewellers and Rodney Wayne Hairdressing. If you have written books or are regularly published, then this can be a huge advantage.

Two issues to consider, however are how it will be used and how it sounds. If you are a one-person operation or if you are your brand (most professional speakers fall into this category) then this can be very successful. However, in a number of cases, the staff of larger concerns will shorten it themselves. For example, one hairdresser at Rodney Wayne's says "I work at Waynes!" If you are happy with this, there is no issue. If you are set on using your own name, consider using just your surname. 'Stephen Johnson Engineers' could be more successful as just 'Johnson Engineers'.

The number of syllables or hyphenation also makes a difference. If your name is Mariana Patterson-Johnson, that's nine syllables – far too many to use. Few will remember it and it's far too long to type into a search engine without the risk of a misspelling or hyphenation error. Similarly, if your name is foreign to the country you want to trade in or is not easily pronounced (as in the Monty Python example), then avoid it. Examples would be Zmudowski and Nasralvhrnec in English speaking countries (real names!).

There is also the longer term issue of selling one day and being happy that the person taking over can still use your name.

Waddington Smyth and Bladdersworth

This is a common format for professional service firms – three principals linked together. Nothing wrong with it, except that you can assume it will be shortened. Deloitte Touche Tohmatsu is usually just Deloittes to clients. It is invariably the third name that disappears, so hopefully no egos will be offended. Two names are better than three, and one name is better than two. In general, it is best to avoid hard to pronounce or difficult to spell names and ones with too many syllables.

Think about the image you convey when there are connotations from a name or when used in combination with others. An example would be the partners of law firm ChanceryGreen (see last chapter) being Sly, Price and Welsh.

Using the conventional surnames format also faces the issue of making you simply look like all the rest, so you are very unlikely to stand out or be terribly memorable.

"Where everyone gets a bargain"

The big box New Zealand store, The Warehouse, uses this headline as a slogan, but it has worked its way into the brand. Whenever you hear the words "The Warehouse" your brain completes the sentence by adding "where everyone gets a bargain". The point here is that a carefully chosen tag line or slogan is just as important, if not more so, than the brand.

Places, loaded words and descriptors

A place name such as Auckland Employment Services or King Street Auto Electrical only works if you have no intention of moving, or it is associated with a well respected location. Personally, I think it is limiting and shows a general lack of imagination, but in some cases can work.

On the negative side, the geographical name may be regarded with suspicion by those outside the area. 'Auckland' may not be well respected by all who are outside of that city, while some areas may be regularly associated with crime, slums or other such negative attributes.

On the positive side, if you are only appealing to locals then associating yourself loud and proud with your city or region can be a huge benefit. It's a simple matter of drawing a line down the centre of a page and listing good points about the defined area on one side and bad points on the other. Then look up a local directory to find all others who use that word to detect possible confusion. It will soon become apparent whether it is a good idea or not.

Other types of brand include loaded words or words with connotations. In the previous section, ChanceryGreen is the brand of a law firm that specialises in environmental law. 'Green' has clear and relevant connotations for this market. Other words can be found that may in part convey the market segment or an attribute of your service, spend time on www.thesaurus.com

A basic descriptor of your service is a non-brand. If you call yourself 'Insurance and Investments', that's almost meaningless as a brand. Sure it describes what you do, but prospective clients will see it as the generic and not the brand. A firm of architects calls themselves 'The Architects'. Imagine one of them phoning a client, "It's John here from The Architects". The client takes it as the generic. Any of their competitors could use that exact statement equally as well. Where is the brand value?

Generics rarely work, so avoid them as your brand. Confine them to a descriptor under the brand.

"I deal with Jack, but someone named John wrote to me"

Remember that people deal with people, so most of your brand building will be at an individual relationship level. I have seen this abused time and time again without the professional concerned realising what she/he is doing.

I met someone trading as 'John Smith Services' yet preferred to be called Jack in conversation, signs his letters 'J K Smith' and in his printed profile is 'John K Smith'!

Decide on ONE of these and use it for the business name, as well as what you are called in conversation and in written material. In his case, he needs to decide between 'Jack Smith Services' and 'Smith Services' for the brand. In all forms of print including his signature, he should be Jack Smith. This is how branding works – by being consistent in its use. So decide who you want to be.

What about 'member of...' type brands?

This is not a brand as such. It is a mark of affiliation. If you are 'Smith Professional Services, member of the Galaxy Group' then it's the same as being 'Smith Builders, Registered Master Builder'. It is unlikely to be the reason a client would choose you but it can certainly help. It helps because just like franchise groups, clients like the safety implication of a higher authority or standard.

Using this sort of affiliate brand can be of value, so long as the affiliate brand has a high profile to your target market in its own right. An example would be 'Master Builders', which as a brand advertises in its own right. This reinforces its value to prospective clients of the membership.

To get the value of the affiliation across to prospective clients, you may need to exaggerate it at first. Make it the lead story in newsletters, list other members, put the affiliate logo on all your marketing material and even write a bit about it in your business card (if there is space). But it will never replace the need to develop your own individual brand.

In summary...

There are only three things to remember:
(1) People buy brands!
(2) People buy brands!
(3) People buy brands!

Make sure you have a clear branding strategy for your firm. It is often best to get an outside perspective on this, so engage a branding agency or some other marketing consultant to facilitate the process of reviewing or coming up with one. The small investment will almost certainly be worth it.

Paul Watkins

Chapter 11
What marketing stuff works and what doesn't?

The mathematics of marketing

40/40/20 is the magic formula. These break down into:

- **40%** of your marketing time and money should be spent on your own existing clients
- **40%** of your marketing time and money should be on other people's clients
- **20%** is the 'lottery' component, that is advertising, web site, general brand awareness and other untargeted activity

The first 40% is often the most overlooked. Existing clients are invariably worth more than they are currently paying. Sometimes called the 'low hanging fruit', they could be using far more of your services or the same ones more often. Most firms devote time to thanking clients for their services, which in itself is a worthwhile exercise, but there should be an active plan for growing the value of the ones you most want more work from.

It is also a fact that ignoring them in your marketing plan will lead to attrition. And following the 40/40/20 formula, if you spend $20,000 on advertising, you should be spending $40,000 on keeping and improving the value of existing clients.

The second 40% can be a very powerful range of activities, whereby you are identifying non-competing firms that have a clientbase that fit your desired type. More on this in a later chapter, but these can be regarded as semi-qualified prospects.

The last 20% is for general advertising or directory listings. Because you cannot control who responds, these can be described as a lottery.

"Only half my advertising works, the problem being I don't know which half"

This famous quote (attributed to more than one person) is not correct for professional services – where almost ALL advertising doesn't work.

In a survey of top performing financial advisers (after all, why would you ask poor performers?) by Canadian marketing consultant Don Pooley, the chart on the next page is a summary of their experiences. The question asked was how effective is each of these techniques in generating new business? Note that the percentage figures do not refer to leads, but to the percentage of leads from that source that turned into revenue generating work. As an example, while the Yellow Pages may generate lots of leads, only 8.7% of these became clients. Similarly 'Contacting Existing Clients' resulted in nearly 70% of such contacts generating new fee paying business.

Source of new business	Success	$$$	Time
Referrals	100%	½$	tttt
Contacting existing clients	69.6%	$	tttt
Seminars, teaching classes	60.9%	$	ttt
Speeches to civic or trade groups	60%	$	tt
Participation in organisations	56.5%	$$	tt
Getting published in the media	43.5%	$$	t
Cold calling by phone / in person	17.4%	$$$	t
Website	17.2%	$$$$	t
Directory listings (Yellow Pages)	8.7%	$$$$	t
Advertising	4.3%	$$$$	t

They have been broken into three groups, as indicated by the background shading, and each of the following three chapters have been devoted to these in turn. But before going on, note that the three groups roughly correspond to the 40/40/20 groupings of activities.

The top group is clearly 'existing clients' and is where 40% of your time and money should be directed. The light shaded group in the middle is the 40% devoted to 'other people's clients' and the bottom darker shaded group is the 20% devoted to advertising; otherwise known as the lottery.

Note that while this was a survey of financial planners, other informal surveys confirm the same results to be true for all professional services.

The '$$$' and the 'ttt' columns

There are two other columns in that chart. The first is '$$$' or the cost of these activities. These dollar signs should be interpreted as relative to the other entries in the same column.

For example, contacting existing clients would include newsletters, posted reminders, campaigns, seminars and other activities that would have a small cost associated with them, but only very small compared to the cost of advertising. Generating referrals has a very small cost (hence the ½ symbol). As a general rule, as you move down the list from very effective to less effective, the cost increases.

The last column refers to time required, or labour content. This increases inversely to cost. The top group of activities such as referrals and giving speeches would clearly take a lot more of your time than just writing out a cheque to a web designer, so there is a hidden cost that must be considered.

It's a balancing act

Clearly you must balance these activities to fit with your personality, type of business and opportunities. Some people shudder at the thought of picking up the phone, taking a client to lunch, giving a speech or asking for a referral. They just want the phone to ring and to spend all day doing what they have been trained to do.

I recall facilitating a marketing workshop for a law firm, the senior partners of which were turning white with shock when it came to discussing asking for referrals. They considered this style of activity, "A blight on our professionalism" and asked that I move on to offer discussion on "more appropriate" marketing activities.

Others live for the people contact and would rather be lunching or chatting to clients all day and delegating most of the actual work. My own accountant used to do this when I owned a retail chain in the late 80s. He would call in unexpectedly for a coffee and we would spend half an hour or more each time discussing ideas for expansion, financial matters about the business and which of his other clients it would be in our interest to meet. Much of our growth can be attributed to these informal discussions.

The bottom line is that it will always be a mixture of activities that create success. However, do not write any of them off until you have considered a way you might do them comfortably, how they fit with other marketing activities and what you would personally prefer to do.

Paul Watkins

Chapter 12
The expensive stuff

The bottom of the 'what works' chart

The chart in the previous chapter lists the worst activities as: Cold calling by phone or in person, Website (when it is just a static online brochure), Directory listings and Advertising. This chapter will take you through why this is the case.

Two ways to find a new wife/husband

Looking for a new husband or wife? Here are two ways to go about finding one, and there are significant marketing message behind them. Peter's approach is to first imagine his ideal partner – age, looks, background and so on. Then he buys an appropriate outfit that he believes would appeal to her. Next he has to find someone like that, so does some research on the bars and nightclubs in town to find one that has patrons most matching the profile of her ideal partner.

Then he picks a good night when the chosen venue will be at its busiest. He walks in and when a person matching the ideal profile is spotted, goes up to her and says, "Hi, I'm Peter, would you like to marry me?" Now he may be turned down (surprise, surprise), but undeterred, goes up to the next one and then the next one proposing marriage in each case. Eventually luck might prevail and the offer is accepted, but maybe not. He could have just wasted the entire night with this approach. If it failed, Peter of course blames the suit manufacturer and the researcher for picking the wrong bar.

Patrick, on the other hand, has a different approach. He has decided to date first. He finds someone through an introduction from a friend, a work colleague or meets them at a social gathering. On the surface she may appear to be very nice so he asks her out on a date. If it goes well, they go on another, then another. After 20 or so dates, they are comfortable with one another and have met each other's families. Finally after a few months of dating, he pops the question.

Now you will be curious by this stage as to what on earth this has to do with marketing. It has a lot to do with how marketing works. Go back to Peter's approach. Assume that he is advertising his services. He determines the ideal profile for a client (partner) then finds the best medium i.e. newspaper, radio etc (bar or nightclub) to get his message across. He then dresses up the offer with a flash advertisement (the suit) and presents himself to the selected audience; going straight up to them and smacking them in the face with the offer – him – this being the equivalent of the prospect seeing the advertisement.

The problem with this approach is that he has to show the advertisement to hundreds or even thousands of people to get any of them to take it up! That's how advertising works. It is literally a lottery. And of course when it doesn't work, you fire the ad agency (blaming the suit).

Now Patrick on the other hand, finds prospects and 'dates' them. He carefully selects qualified individual prospects through networking, referrals and other people's clients. He invites her to find out about his services through a personalised and very relevant direct mail piece. He then phones or invites her to a seminar he is running. This allows each party to find out about each other. He gets her to meet his 'family' by telling them about other services and then eventually asks for the order. (This concept was first written about by Seth Godin)

The first meeting is unlikely to give you the results you are after, it's just like a first date. But be clear in your objectives; don't leave the meeting hanging in space with no go-forward goal. It should be something like to meet again, send a formal proposal or have no further contact.

Being introduced to you by referral is like a friend setting you up for a bind date. While you might hate bind dates, you trust the friend so are prepared to go along with an open mind. And since asking them to marry you on the first date is going to be less successful than after a few dates, you need a 'dating strategy', so keep in touch. They need time to learn to trust you.

If you want to turn away potential clients, just let your ego do the talking

If you saw an advertisement that read, "Acknowledged leaders in trademark law" or "When ou need the best" or "Our designs just keep winning awards" or "Number one in residential house sales", what crosses your mind? Blowhard, big head, yeah, right, whatever!

What does NOT enter your mind is 'Wow, I must pick them because they sound so good!' Telling the world you are good lacks credibility. It is simply an ego trip on the part of the provider or the CEO of the firm. I'm sure that last sentence offended a few readers, but many such statements in advertising are often designed to annoy rival firms as much as to impress potential customers. This is not a good motive.

Such statements lack credibility when used as the main argument in advertising. The world is far too full of awards, superlatives and exaggerations for any of them to really have any impact. Pick up any DVD movie and read: "An instant classic". "The greatest love story ever told" or "Without doubt, a true masterpiece" on the cover. All of these are meaningless and lacking in any information on which you can base a judgement. After all, why don't the number one real estate agents in your area get ALL the listings?

But wait, you say. You said that the key argument of this book is for you to be 'number one'. Yes, that's right. But that will not be achieved through advertising, where you allow your ego to dictate the headline. Being "number one" is earned.   As a footnote, awards can successfully be used as support statements jus as "member of..." in promotional material, but not as the headline or main reason clients would choose you.

www.clichés-r-us.com

There is no such web site as this, but it sure sounds like this is where most slogans or 'statements of client commitment' are found. Ask any professional service firm for their statement and then put any other firm's name in front of it – regardless of the service offered – and it will still fit. An example:

> *"We are absolutely committed to meeting the service expectations of our clients by finding cost-effective solutions in such a way that they will readily acknowledge our firm as the best possible provider of such services."*

What meaningless drivel! Try to find a firm that would NOT want such a sentiment implied in their service provision. While it may (although I doubt it) have some meaning internally, it has no impact on the outside world.

"You can expect rain on Sunday..."

Advertising professional services is like listening to a weather report. You know there is some basis to the claims, but there is also a lot of doubt. Perhaps there is a 60% chance of it being right – just slightly more likelihood of right than wrong. This is how advertising of professional services is viewed. You are trying to advertise a promise, a maybe. You are saying we-will-try-really-hard-for-you but, we can only offer you a slightly better than 50/50 chance of the desired outcome. This is why successful advertising of professional services is so difficult.

Compare it to an advertisement that reads, "43 inch Sony LCD TV $1.990" has no ambiguity. You know exactly what you are getting, the brand, size and cost. And implied in all new electronics is a warranty, so if it fails you return it for repair or replacement. And of course you can scan the advertising of rival retailers to compare prices. So how do you do this for professional services? You can't for the firm, so don't try!

So, should you advertise at all?

Probably not. There would be little need if you follow the other ideas in this book. However there will be rare times when it may be a good idea to advertise a specific service, if it is clearly defined, easily understood and perhaps at a fixed price.

But what about phone directories?

Yes you need a listing in key directories. Many of those that look you up will be existing clients who don't remember your contact details, so don't expect it to be a key source of new business – unless you don't care who contacts you.

Advertising is a lottery – you have no idea who is going to call and in many cases they will be tyre-kickers or time wasters. One lawyer told me how he ran the headline 'Family Trusts' in his Yellow Pages phone directory advert. He said he regularly got calls from undesirable people saying, "My family is in trouble and it says I can trust you.' Point made!

Make sure your directory listings include your web site, a generic email contact, phone, fax, and cell phones for key personnel if you don't mind after hours contact. Make it as easy as possible to for clients to contact you.

And one final point on this subject. My new phone directory turned up more than six months ago and it still remains in its plastic delivery bag. When I mentioned this to friends it turns out they rarely, if ever, use paper phone books either (we all use the online versions), so this brings up the issue of what sort of listing (size and cost) do you really need, which once again depends on your chosen target market.

Appreciating that many people search directories online, perhaps listing under multiple categories, based on specific services or target clients, could be a good idea.

Ignore the Internet at your peril

As of late 2007, total time spent in front of Internet screens and games consoles exceeded time watching TV in the western world for the first time. While this cross over is a significant statistic in its own right, it also signals something else.

The key difference between TV and the Internet/games consoles is the level of interactivity. TV is static. You watch the programmes at scheduled times and your level of interactivity is limited to laughing or crying. The Internet and console games are user-prescribed content. Click on a button or key and the screen changes or the characters move as you wish them to.

Internet content is now almost unlimited. It's practically impossible to think of a topic or area of knowledge that is not on a web site somewhere. Nearly 85% of all households in developed countries now have access to the Internet. Look at the explosive growth of online banking and social networking sites like Facebook.

Why your website maybe a waste of time

Once up on a time all you have to do was put up a simple web site that was basically your brochure. It had the standard button, 'About Us', 'Services', 'contact Us' and perhaps 'Testimonials'. To get traffic you simply identified key words and made sure you overused them in your text.

But then life changed. Web sites now look and work different. How we search for them has changed and Search Engine Optimisation (SEO) has gone through radical change. Add to this the fact that over 50% of all searches are performed on phones or tablets.

You want a new TV, so you search for reviews or Consumer rankings on the 'best'. Once you are happy you know exactly what you want, you then look up a price comparison site to see who has it at the cheapest price. Then one evening, you have been phoned by an insurance provider and while the offer to see you sounds ok, you immediately look them up on your tablet and see exactly who they are.

We live our lives on the Internet. We bank, shop, keep up with news, entertain ourselves and work on it. As a result it has become so much a part of our lives that we rarely do anything without consulting its immense database of knowledge. And it's exactly the same for professional services. My GP recently told me that she is heartily sick of her patients arriving with a piece of paper printed from the Internet, and beginning the conversation with "I think what is wrong with me is…"

Content is king

A term you will frequently hear in relation to web sites is that 'content is king!' A website's content, far more so than its products or services, is what attracts visitors. Do you provide a reason for people to spend more than a few seconds reading your pages? Do you offer something of genuine value, something that will enlighten or inform them or make them think, 'wow, this person really does know what they are talking about'? By the way, if you can't write good content yourself, get someone to write it for you – it's definitely worth the investment.

Creating great content

So what does this valuable content look like? Start by asking yourself what a visitor would learn from reading it. Will it tell them what to look for or be wary of when engaging someone offering your services? This is how you must think about your content. Web site visitors do not want to be sold to, they want to LEARN!

Some good ideas for content include Frequently Asked Questions (FAQs). It should be easy to run up say 10 questions that your clients frequently ask you and offer one paragraph answers. A bonus of this sort of content is that each question then becomes searchable in its own right. The single most popular search term on the Internet is "How to…" with the sentence completed with whatever the searcher is wanting to know. So if some of your questions started with, "How to get the best deal on a mortgage" or "How to make sure your architect is the right one for you". This helps the chances of being found. You can then link the answers to relevant services you offer on other pages on your site. This way your valuable information subtly links to a sale pitch.

In case you are worried about it, you're not giving away your expertise for free by doing this. Your prospective clients will still work with you, no matter how detailed you get. Their impression will be that you clearly know what you are talking about.

A Golden Rule with content is to keep it FRESH! The easiest way to do this is to run a blog. This is like a diary of your thoughts. There are no rules as to the frequency, but monthly is a good start. Write maybe two paragraphs each time on a topical subject. It could be anything from the list already discussed. It can also be articles from your newsletter. It doesn't have to be a revolutionary new item each time, just an update. For example, you may publish an article entitled, "How to get the best mortgage deal out of your bank" and then six months later add a new one called, "The NEW rules for getting the best mortgage deal out of your bank".

Search Engine Optimization

Being found! Sometimes abbreviated to SEO, Internet users almost never search beyond the first page of search engine results for any given search query, so when your website does not appear on that first page, the chances of anyone finding your website through a search engine becomes next to nothing.

SEO is a very difficult thing to get right and as soon as you do, Google change the rules on you! If you are serious about getting high rankings, then you need to engage an SEO specialist. Such firms typically charge a few hundred dollars a month to maintain your rankings, so you would need to build this into your annual marketing budget.

However there are things you can do yourself that make a difference. This is a big topic in itself, but the best advice is to go to Youtube and type in, "How to get better search rankings 2014". There are literally thousands of videos on this subject. Make sure you include the current year as the rules change so often that you need to be up-to-date on current thinking.

As discussed in a previous section, content is the big secret. Adding new content regularly and keeping it topical will have the search engines finding you.

Finding a competent web designer

How do you choose a competent web designer when it appears that everyone from age 12 upwards can make one! The answer is to know what to ask them. Find out what they have done in the past. Ask for two or three previous clients that you can call as referees. Ask them what their philosophies are on Search Engine Optimization and design. What are the trends they have observed?

It's a matter of being comfortable that they understand your requirements and that you are happy that they can deliver. When it comes to price, there are no set fees in the industry, but a good site with multiple pages can cost a few thousand dollars.

Audi Vs BMW

One of my previous cars was an Audi. When a friend first saw it he didn't recognise the car. I then discovered after a while that a number of people didn't recognise it.

When discussing this with someone he told me a great story. He said if you stop at an intersection in a BMW and 10 pedestrians are waiting to cross the road, eight out of the 10 will recognise and admire it as a BMW. But if you drive up to the same set of lights in an Audi, only two of the 10 will recognise it. But they will be the RIGHT two people!

In marketing terms, widespread public brand recognition and huge numbers of people knowing who you are don't matter. It's that the RIGHT people know.

Cold calling

For professional services – you must be joking! A handful of firms offer a service or product that lends itself to cold calling, and do so very successfully, but it's a very small handful.

"The more people you reach the more likely it is that you're reaching the wrong people." – *Seth Godin*

Paul Watkins

Chapter 13
Now the stuff that matters

The stuff in the middle

From the chart of activities again, the items in the middle are:
- Seminars, teaching classes
- Speeches to civic or trade groups
- Participation in organisations of potential clients
- Getting published

This is the stuff that matters. Advertising may have limited and only supporting impact, but this chapter deals with the stuff that makes the real difference. It will be clear from this list that these are all about educating your target market and gaining credibility, for both you and your firm.

She's in the paper so must be expert!

Nothing creates credibility and profile as fast as being published. This includes the press, TV, magazines and writing books. This is because readers think that the press wouldn't have quoted you if they didn't see you as a credible commentator on that subject.

Remember to reduce the size of the pond before you approach the Media

Whatever community you live in there will be one main paper and a number of smaller papers. Getting quoted in the main one will be the most difficult, but also not necessary. Remember that you only need to be quoted to your target audience, which comes from finding that smaller pond.

So once you have identified your target niche, then find out what media they read or watch or listen to. For example, your target niche may be the motor trade. They will probably have an industry publication from their own trade association and subscribe to one or two other magazines or web sites. Your goal is to be published in these and not worry about the mainstream media. You can dominate the media relevant to your niche by offering topical articles and perhaps an "Ask the Expert" Q&A section for readers to write in.

A quick point on the media. Electronic media (web sites) is fast taking over the traditional domain of the printed press. Don't ignore this as web sites could well be read far more than magazines or printed matter for your targeted niche. This will vary considerably from niche to niche, so make sure you take the time to understand the niche. To find out which magazines they read or web sites they visit, ask your clients already in your targeted niche. Take one or two to lunch or when you visit their office take note of what magazines and industry newsletters they get. Be blatant about it by asking. Tell them that you are keen to develop an expertise to their industry and therefore which publications should you be trying to get into. If they are a good client, they will be more than happy to tell you.

They need you like you need them!

Before I cover the specifics of approaching the chosen media, remember that they need you as much as you need them. They produce a regular publication that relies on a constant stream of interesting reader-relevant information and topical articles. This is where you can be of great value to them – by providing that content.

Approaching your targeted Media

First step – understand the publication. Read a few issues of the trade magazine or web site or newsletter or journal. Get a feel for the type of articles they feature, the topics, the style of writing, the length, the photographs and the various sections.

Then decide if you are capable of writing it or if you need help from someone who does it for a living. There is an art to writing for the media and spending a few hundred dollars on a freelance journalist or PR person can be extremely worthwhile. They will know how to quote you, how to attach an attention grabbing headline and how to de-jargonise it for the less educated readers. Of great importance is that experienced writers can make it sound genuinely news-worthy and not read like an advertisement.

Most industry publications and free newspapers or web sites have few if any staff writers. Many have just an editor and then a bunch of contributors on a freelance or contracted basis. This is why a well written piece that is consistent with their style will usually be printed.

Note that they will always reserve the editorial rights meaning that they may edit or re-write pieces of it without your permission. Quite often they will change the headline or take out any passages that read too much like an advertisement.

So once you have written it, phone the editor and tell them that you have something you feel would be of interest to his/her readers. In 99% of the cases, they will tell you to send it in but offer no guarantees of it being included. That's all you want. If it has been written well and has a quality accompanying picture of you, the chances of it getting put in are very high.

Don't sell – educate

Just before you watch the six o'clock news on New Zealand's TV One each night, you will see a two-minute program called 'Food in a Minute'. It shows you how to use tins of baked beans, peaches, frozen peas and other products from a processed food manufacturer. It has been a huge success for the company. And if you tune into TV after midnight or mid-morning, you can enjoy a raft of 30 minute infomercials. These are also highly successful, selling truckloads of kitchen appliances, weight loss program and exercise machines.

Why are they so successful? Because they EDUCATE the customer about the product or service. The two-minute food item shows how the product can be used to make quick meals. In fact the brand and product are secondary to the message – but integral to the recipe. This puts the product into context and shows how it can have a positive impact on your life.

This is why being published works. It allows you to put your services into context through case studies, industry relevant commentary, checklists, examples, questionnaires, explanations in lay terms or putting it in ways that the potential client would not have thought of. To be seen as the expert, you need to demonstrate your expertise in a form that your target market can relate to.

Are your pens aircraft-safe?

An item in the media reported that jeans manufacturer Levi Strauss has launched a line of jeans with "anti-radiation" pockets, which are a hit with customers. The Communications Manager for Levi's says, "We are not implying in any way that mobile phones are dangerous..." Yeah, right! Radiation can cause sterility, so a radiation emitting cell phone in your pocket is not a totally desirable option – which customers know because these jeans are selling well.

Similarly there were signs at airports for Uni pens, promoting them as "the first aircraft-safe pens". The posters explained: "will not react to aircraft pressurisation and leak in your pocket" Is this for real?

The interesting point about these examples is that consumers would never have considered them issues until the advertisers brought them up. They were created to cause consumers to doubt the brands they currently use or to think carefully before choosing jeans. This is what you want. Otherwise you have no point of differentiation. In your own efforts to educate your target market, think of how your service could be put in terms of a previously unknown fear. This can be a key method in generating more business from existing clients.

Tell me WHY, not WHAT

New Zealand based, Bayleys Real Estate, ran an advertisement that features two guys hitchhiking. One is holding up a sign that says the place name. Right beside it is the same chap holding a similar sign, but this time is says the destination as well as the line "for mum's birthday". Which one would you be more inclined to pick up?

Now the interesting bit is that when you come to tell others about what you did, for the first one you might say "I picked up a hitchhiker today". In the second case you might say "I picked up a young chap trying to get home for his mother's birthday today". BIG difference! In the first case you might never think of the guy again, but in the second you are likely to start wondering how the birthday went and imagining how pleased his mother would have been that her son had made the effort.

Be honest with yourself – who really wants your service? Is it a highly desirable engagement or a grudge purchase? No one says, "Wow, isn't it exciting, I'm going to town to spend thousands with my lawyer today." If clients could live their lives without your service, they would! So the answer is to stop selling your product or service and sell its purpose. Women do not pay out thousands to Weight Watchers to lose weight (perhaps a few do) – they are buying increased self-esteem. Most people do not join Toastmasters to learn how to speak better in public; they join to give themselves a boost in personal confidence.

Ask yourself – WHY they would want to use your service and that becomes your headline. As a client I don't care WHAT you do, but I do care about how it will enhance my life.

Tell me a story

The two adverts on the next two pages are for lump sum trauma (critical illness) insurance. The second one is considerably longer than the first but tells a compelling story based around the consequences of not having trauma insurance. The first one simply tells you the facts – all quite correct, but nothing compelling. TELL A STORY! Make it real for the reader. Have them part of the tragedy or the triumphs around your services.

A lump sum in the event of a critical illness

The real tragedy of a debilitating illness like cancer, a stroke or heart attack comes after you recover. The financial impact from a serious illness can be severe and add debt, temporarily stop your income and cut into your retirement savings.

But all of this can be avoided with a trauma or critical illness policy that gives you a lump sum upon diagnosis of the disease.

Call us now for a no obligation quote on the amount of cover appropriate to your circumstances

888-8888 or visit www.maxcover.co.nz

MAX COVER BROKERS

A tale of two sisters

Carrie and Anne were both 42 year-old mothers of three, on incomes of $50,000 and with husbands on incomes of $80,000. Both families had mortgages of $280,000. Both also had $50,000 saved for retirement, accumulated from regular salary deductions.

One unfortunate day Carrie and Anne were both diagnosed with breast cancer. They had to give up work to endure the treatment and their respective husbands also had to take long periods of time off to look after the children and attend to their wives while recovering. Carrie had health insurance, so was able to choose the hospital and get immediate attention, while Anne endured the public system.

Carrie also had a 'trauma' insurance policy, which paid her a lump sum of $250,000 upon diagnosis of a serious illness such as cancer. This more than compensated for the lost income. In fact there was also enough to make a substantial payment on the mortgage and put a sum aside for future emergencies because from the time of the claim, she was no longer insurable.

Anne was not so fortunate. While her treatment was also successful, she had lost a year's pay and her husband had lost four months income. They came out of the treatment with their retirement savings of $50,000 cashed in and their mortgage increased by $30,000 to make up for the lost income, child care expenses and medical costs. Now 43, Carrie and Anne still have 22 years working life ahead of them (assuming retirement at 65) and have picked up their lives where they left off.

Anne and her husband started their super fund again from zero, saving at the previous rate of $600 per month; They would have about $270,000 saved at 65. Not bad, but that extra $30,000 on the mortgage would cost them another $43,000 in interest along the way.

Carrie on the other hand had the trauma policy payment, which replaced all the lost income, paid $100,000 off the mortgage and put $70,000 into an interest bearing investment for future major medical issues. As a result their mortgage was paid off 12 years earlier and with the mortgage payments from that point on redirected into the retirement fund (along with the $600 per month they didn't have to stop) they would retire with the princely sum of $1.05 million! Quite a difference to say the least.

If you would like to find out if trauma insurance is right for you, please call us 888-8888 or find out more at www.maxcover.co.nz

Advertisement for Max Cover Brokers

Where do they congregate? Find out and then offer to talk to them

You will find that your desired type of client tends to congregate. They form clusters with others of a similar mindset or interests, such as industry associations, networking groups, sports clubs and community groups. Offer yourself as a speaker to such groups. Present for 15 minutes, giving your speech a name like:

- '5 critical facts to know about the law before going into business.'
- 'Before you travel, which bits should you book on the Internet and which are safer through a travel agent?'
- 'Taking the stress out of working with an architect.'
- 'If you think working with some trades-people can be frustrating, wear the shoes of the tradesperson!'
- 'The surprising truth about which home improvements add value and which that don't.'

As you can see , it should be a catchy title (don't worry about how long it is) and communicate a clear educational benefit that the audience will gain from hearing the short speech.

Some of the mechanics of speaking

Practice, practice, practice. Never just go along and wing it. It will be obvious if you do. Have it peer reviewed beforehand by someone else in your firm or even better by someone who is outside your firm, the later being able to tell you if you have used too much jargon.

Avoid using PowerPoint as it's too clumsy, too subject to failure and few venues will be set up to accommodate it. In rare cases you may have to if you need to show them pictures to illustrate a point, but try to avoid it. Style it as a casual jargon-free talk to a small but highly-targeted group.

Do NOT hand out promotional material, brochures of business cards. It is designed to educate the audience and position you as the expert. If it sounds like an advertisement they will be put off and it could even backfire, so don't say things like 'my office hours are...' or 'I am available to members if they want to make an appointment...' Have business cards on hand but only give them out if asked.

Use humour if you are comfortable doing so and observe the normal rules of avoiding anything that may be offensive, such as political, sexual or religious references. The Internet has literally tens of thousands of one-liners about almost every profession so find a few that you can slip in where appropriate.

If you are serious about this as a promotional tool, join a Toastmasters group and have it reviewed by members or seek out a speaking coach (contact a Speaker's Bureau for names). This will teach you the importance of eye contact, gestures, how to use your voice to maximum effect, how to have a catchy opening, the general construction of the speech and how to end it in a non-sales way that generates business.

Done well, this can be an extremely powerful technique for creating credibility and help make you stand out within your profession. It could even lead to paid speaking engagements.

"I'm attending a course on the subject – much better than any seminar"

We are seminar-ed to death at times and getting the attendance you are after is not always easy. So to make it sound much more appealing, offer a 'course'. A course makes it sound more like they will genuinely learn something. It could be a 2-part lunchtime course, a 4-part breakfast course or a 6-part course in the evenings at a local school.

Take it one step further – offer it online or mail based. Most western cultures have a do-it-yourself mentality, so use this to your advantage.

Remember, it's all about trust

Think about the last few sections you just read. If selling professional services is all about selling that great intangible called trust, then listening to an 'expert' talk about it in a full 15 minute uninterrupted speech or reading about it in a quarter page press or magazine article must be better than 25 hard hitting words in an advertisement. This is why the techniques we are discussing now work.

Paul Watkins

Chapter 14
Talk to the ones you already know!

The low-hanging fruit

Existing clients are best referred to as the low-hanging fruit. You already have a relationship with them, so extending it to generate more business is a much, much easier task than finding a brand new client. They will read anything you send them, respond to invitations (even if it's a 'no') and if you ask them about themselves, they will almost always answer truthfully.

So while that's easy to say, how do you do it in a manner that doesn't cost much, doesn't take up too much time and is known to work. That is the subject of this chapter. The case study below explains how one law firm did it, which is part 2 of the law firm in the case study in Chapter 4.

Back to the law firm with 5,500 clients you met in Chapter 4

This issue of where their business was generated from came as a revelation to the partners, and they also realised that they never contacted clients; simply waited for phone calls.

They readily saw that the opportunity for cross-selling was huge and agreed that strategic alliances should be established with complimentary services. They advertised regularly for new clients but did nothing to communicate to the current client-base. So what did they do?

1. They gave themselves 12 months to contact every client (500 per month or 25 per day) and enter them onto a segmented database based on six key segments.

2. The data entered would include a number of items not currently known e.g. for business clients, how many staff they have, do they own investment property and so on. Very few refused to answer the questions.

3. A client communication strategy has been adopted, including a quarterly newsletter in two variations – one for business clients, one for individuals. 1,000 selected clients receive it.

4. All external advertising apart from a small phone directory listing has stopped. Advertising dollars have

been directed towards reactivating their current client base instead.

5. Active cross-selling strategies have been developed, based on a campaigned checklist covering all of a client's possible legal requirements.

The magic of 90-day contact

FACT: Increasing the frequency of client contact increases retention rates and sales. US research house, Customer Development Corporation, found the following results for an insurance company's clients, one year after they were first acquired.

- Without any contact, only 43% of clients were retained.
- Retention jumped to 82% (nearly double!) for those with four or more points of contact during the year.

Contacting clients every 90-days is not an arbitrary number. Four times a year is the MINIMUM number of points of contact to maintain a 'relationship'. Any less is simply a passing acquaintance. Without going into lengthy explanations, it is all explained in detail in the book, "How to get new business in 90 days and keep it forever" by Wendy Evans. It works. And 90-day contact is most easily and cost-effectively achieved via a quarterly newsletter.

Increased contact = increased sales

Tell them what you do over and over again, because they forget. More importantly, don't just tell them WHAT you do; tell them WHY they need you. Put it in context. Don't say "I can do the design work on any renovations you have planned", say "If you really like the location, why shift? Renovations such as adding a room may not be as expensive as you think and that way you get your next house at the same location!" Get the idea? Tell them why.

And the more you tell them the more they come to believe it. LL Bean, the huge US mail order company changed the frequency of mailing their catalogues from quarterly to monthly. Sales skyrocketed. Joe Girard, the 'world's greatest car salesman', sent a postcard to every customer every month. The bottom line – contact them over and over and over again, reminding them how you can be of value.

And remember that it is cumulative. The first time you contact them, you may not have talked to them for some time – perhaps even years – so you can't expect them to instantly respond. The second time may give better results, the third time even more and so on. It's like re-discovering an old girl friend. It takes a few dates to reignite the flame.

Quarterly newsletters can do it

The easiest way to meet the 90-day contact rule is with a quarterly newsletter. It can contain case studies of work you have done, introduce new staff members and talk about key changes to your industry that might affect them. Remember to make every article relevant to them as clients.

Two sides of an A4/letter sheet is fine, four pages also works, but no need to do them longer than that. It is incredibly difficult to keep their attention even with just two pages, so keep it short. Short and frequent is better than long and infrequent.

"They pigeon-holed me"

A project management firm undertook two contracts for a local authority, managing the construction of two separate workshops. The firm then got nothing more from the local authority for nearly a year, which surprised the owner as he thought he had done a good job.

So he phoned to ask if there were any future projects that he should consider being a bidder for. They said, "We don't have any more workshops in the wind." He realised that he had pigeon-holed himself as the 'workshop guy'.

He started writing bi-monthly newsletters to key staff inside three local authorities. It went in individually addressed envelopes to about a dozen staff in each, identified as ones he thought could be in positions of influence. The newsletters profiled other projects he was working on, introduced his key staff and gave hints on how to work with project managers.

Shortly after the second one was posted, he received a request for proposal for the management of a job. After the third newsletter, he was asked the same for a project from a neighbouring council – neither of them being workshops.

It could well be just a timing issue

Imagine that you receive a flyer in your letterbox offering lounge suites for half price. What a bargain! $6,000 leather suites for just

$3,000. But what if you had bought a new one just a year ago? They last up to 10 years, so while it's a bargain, it's of no relevance to you as the timing was wrong.

Now change the situation. You have just moved into a new house and decide that a new lounge suite would be nice. Black leather with two recliner chairs. So you plan to visit a few furniture shops in the coming weekend, when that day a flyer arrives offering a FREE coffee table with every leather lounge suite. That's a $600 free gift with the $6,000 suite you want. So you go straight down and buy it. Why did the $3,000 discount not excite as much as what amounts to a 10% discount? Because the first offer was made at the wrong time for you.

You may contact your clientbase with an offer and get a disappointing result. This does not mean that contacting them is a waste of time; it could just mean that the offer may not have been relevant to the recipients at that particular point in time.

Chapter 15
Referrals

The difference between a good adviser and a great advisor is referrals

This is well known within financial service circles. You only get referrals if you deserve them and have a method of asking for them – be it subtle or blatant. This chapter and the next will deal with referrals. In fact I have given it two chapters since it's so important.

Never ask a C-client for a referral

Why? Because they may give you one! The goal of referrals is to replicate good clients, not bad ones. Everything you read from this point is with a view to getting referrals from A and B clients.

The hard task of asking for referrals

According to one US study 86% of surveyed clients would refer their insurance broker to their friends, yet only 12% were asked. I presented at a conference of professional service providers a while ago and asked for an honest answer to the question, 'how many of you regularly ask clients for a referral?' Less than 5% of the room put their hands up and even then I think one or two shouldn't have. When I asked the rest of the room why they didn't, the answers included, "What if the client says no? I'll feel embarrassed." "It's unprofessional." "It's too sales-focused and not client-focused." "It might put them off me" "I wouldn't know how to ask." "It sounds like I'm a door-to-door salesperson", and many others along these lines.

Referrals are universally acknowledged as the best way to get new business and the most frequent question I am asked is how to get more. It's not easy. It's very hard to ask for them without it sounding contrived and at times making the client feel embarrassed or uncomfortable. So this chapter is a collection of methods, some subtle and some blatant, as used successfully by professional service providers. Among them you are sure to find one or two that you will feel comfortable using.

Referral 'rules of engagement'

While there are literally dozens of ways to ask for a request, there are three 'rules' to keep in the back of your mind.
1. Deserve a referral! An average job doesn't deserve a referral. One that exceeded expectations does.

2. Give them every opportunity or method to refer you and make them easy to use.
3. Recognise their efforts. Reward your referrers – and not just with money or gifts.

Why don't you tip every waiter?

You go into Aaron's Café with a client and take a seat in a nice sunny spot. The waiter comes over and says, "Hello there" immediately handing out the menus. "The fish today is salmon. I'll leave these with you and come back soon" He then walks away while you contemplate range on offer. The anonymous waiter returns after five minutes and asks, "Have you decided what you would like?" and proceeds to take the order as requested by you and your companion. It arrives on time and you leave spending $35 for the two of you.

The next day, you take another client to Bob's Café and sit in a suitable sunny spot. John enthusiastically bounces over and while pouring some water says, "Greetings guests, you've chosen a great spot here. My name's John and before I hand out the menus, I've been watching the chef make the Cajun chicken salad this morning and it is definitively my pick of what's on offer today. Now I assume that this is a business lunch so can I ask if you have a time limit or do you want a nice relaxed 90-minute, an enough-time-to-get-the-sale lunch? By the way, which of you is the client and which is the one wants to sell something?" You both have a chuckle at this.

"I'm the client", says your companion. "Great", replies John who turns to you and says, "Since you're the one with the credit card, I'll give you the wine menu. Did you know that wine increases the chance of sale by 38%!" You both laugh again and then you say,

"Thank you, and we don't really have a strict time limit." John leaves and returns after a few minutes.

You both order the Cajun chicken salad (I wonder why). John says "And will you be starting with bread and dips, perhaps a small bowl of Greek salad to compliment it?" "Ah…yeah, sure" you reply. "And the wine, one glass will not be enough for the time you are going to be here, so since you will be having two each, you save money by buying a bottle. Have you chosen one?" He then leans over towards you, points to a wine and says in a loud whisper "This one here is excellent and will taste a lot more expensive than it really is – your client will be impressed" More laughter and you order from the list.

John leaves with the food and wine orders After you finish the main, he turns up unexpectedly with two chocolate covered strawberries on a small pate. Once again in a loud whisper, he says to you "If he hasn't bought yet, the strawberries usually do it" and makes a much exaggerated winking gesture as he leaves.

Perhaps you think John's approach is too over the top – you may even say embarrassing. But the lunch guests spent $75 that day – and they gave John a substantial tip. Better still, they talked about it to a large number of friends.

As a regular guest to the café myself, when I say to friends and colleagues, "I am usually served by this amazing guy who actually sits at the table with us to take our order", I often get "I know who you mean!" Many of the regular guests at that café ask to be served by John and since John has been working there, the average sale per table has gone up nearly 50%. If a waiter can do it – you can.

So why is John so successful?

Repeated studies show that it is not timely service, good food or a smile that encourages restaurant guests to tip, in fact poor service often gets the same small number of tips. The reason some waiters get lots of tips, however, is that they are capable of making the guest feel special. They remember them from a previous visit, pass a compliment, crack a joke, whisper a 'for your ears only' comment about the menu, and so on. It's not hard to do this, regardless of your profession.

Contrast the two comments, "I did some digging on your behalf due to your special circumstances and have come up with..." with the comment, "I regularly come across clients in your circumstances so have a solution for you..." Using the second one is probably intended to make it sound like you are very experienced at this sort of work, but comes across as if you are just putting them into 'Standard Solution B'. The first one makes them feel special. This is what makes you referrable.

Who exactly are you asking for?

If you were an architect, consider these two questions you could ask a client:
(a) "Do you know anyone else that I could be of value to?"
(b) "Just like yourselves, do you have any friends who are considering building a beach house?"

In the case of the first question you are asking them to think of literally anyone, while in the later, they are being asked to identify specific friends in specific circumstances – the same circumstances as they are in. Similarly, an accountant could ask "Just like yourselves, do you know others who have recently started in business?"

The technique here is not just to ask about referrals, but referrals in the same circumstances as the client you just helped. People hang out with the same kind of people as themselves, so are almost guaranteed to know someone like them. This also allows them to identify exactly how you can help these friends so it will appear to them to be a genuine favour. Just asking, "Do you know anyone?" doesn't give the client any reference point to focus on. Most could probably list 60 or even 100 friends or work colleagues who you could potentially help – and really want to, but are unlikely to give you any names at all as their minds can't focus on anyone.

This technique is consistent with the concept of being the **big fish**. You would only ask clients you want to replicate and then get them to identify similar people by specifying them.

How do 2,350 other professionals do it?

'Business by Referral' is a book by Misner and Davis which includes the results of a survey that asked 2,350 business professionals to rate their most successful referral techniques. The results, in order of success rate, were:
1. Networking groups
2. Ask orally
3. Ask in writing
4. Offering incentives
5. Seminars/Speaking

Nothing else ranked as well, so these are the five that matter. The next few sections will cover these in more detail, but it would pay to use more than one to generate a constant flow of referrals. Which ones depend to a large extent on your style of business and your personal preference.

Networking groups

BNI, BoB Clubs, Chamber of Commerce Business After 5s, Internet based networks and other variations exist purely for the purposes of swapping referrals. They have either formal or informal structures that provide the opportunity to swap leads. Many have only one member per profession.

You will find as many members think they are brilliant as a business generator as the number that thinks they are a waste of time. This is because it is necessary to take the time to understand exactly how they work and how to take advantage of them from your perceptive. If you just turn up and go through the motions, then of course they will be a waste of time. I have met a few people who rely almost entirely on the networking club for their new clients as they have figured out how to use it properly.

A consideration is the time commitment as they are usually weekly breakfast clubs and then there is the time required to visit member's businesses to gain a firsthand understanding of how they work. Other considerations are the mix of members and whether this suits your personality or client type. You must give to receive, so while referrals may flow your way, you must give referrals back the other way – or the ones to you will stop! Ensure that you are comfortable doing this before joining.

Some networking groups may not have networking as the primary motive for joining, but can work well anyway. These include Rotary, Lions, Toastmasters, Jaycees, Lyceum and Zonta, as they are full of professionals like yourself.

A seminar designed to attract referrals

I'm sure many of you have run seminars and in the invitation you have included the line "If you know anyone else that may be interested, please bring them along". And no one else turned up! Here is a variation told to me by a professional who says it works very well indeed.

Rather than a straight invitation, change it to a request for what they would like to see you run as a topic. This is a great way to start a new year as it's an excuse the get in touch with good clients in its own right and asks for their opinion – which people love to be asked. The idea is to ask them for seminar topics and then asking if anyone else should be added to the list to get invitations. There is an example of how the invitation could look for an accountant on the next two pages. The topics you list should be relevant to your clients and ones you know you could get a good speaker for. These are just examples.

This is also quite genuine market research. You will be more confidant of running relevant seminars and getting higher attendances. And remember that these are being sent to existing clients, so recipients will certainly read it and the response is generally good.

Date
CName SName
Address
Address

Dear CName

May I ask you your opinion please?

We are planning to run client seminars in the coming year and are keen to make sure that the topics are the ones that clients want to know more about. Could I ask you to take a couple of minutes to fill in the brief questionnaire attached and return it in the enclosed post-paid envelope?

We have also left spaces for you to fill in any other topics that may not be listed. As you know we have strong links within the other professional services so would be confident that we could source an acknowledged expert on the indicated topic.

The results of this survey will be apparent to you in the invitations you receive for the seminars.

I appreciate your time with this.

Regards,

Peter Professional

P.S. You may have friends or colleagues who you think would like to be on the invitation list to some of the seminars. There is space for their details should you like to note them down.

Which seminar topics would most interest you

☐ Investment strategies for retirement
☐ Succession and exit strategies
☐ Gold, antiques and fine art as investments
☐ Family trusts – the pros and cons
☐ Managing business debt to your advantage
☐ Marketing and branding strategies for growth

Preferred time of day:
       7:00am to 8:30am (breakfast provided)
       5:30pm to 7:00pm (drinks and nibbles)
       7:30pm to 9:00pm (light supper provided)

Please add the following people to the seminar invitation list – on the understanding that they will not be approached as prospective clients, just receive the invitations.
Name: ____ _____
Address or email: _____

Name: ____ _____
Address or email: _____

Name: ____ _____
Address or email: _____

Please post to PO Box 8888 in the enclosed envelope or Fax to 999-9999 or email your thoughts to xxx@ABC accountants.com

Never waste a lunch

The great business guru, Tom Peters, wrote a profound statement in one of his books that has been hugely successful to me in my own endeavours. He said "Never waste a lunch". Sometimes the best ideas are almost too simple and have been in front of our noses all along, yet we just couldn't see them.

We work approximately 225 days a year. Each day you have lunch, be it a formal sit down affair or simply a sandwich at your desk. Whatever form it takes, it is down-time from our work – but it doesn't have to be. Turn it into productive time by having lunch with someone of value to you or your business. Tom added, "How often do you get a relaxed 30 minutes with someone that could advantage you, for just $30?"

We all know that the best business done at conferences is the stuff discussed over a beer after the formal sessions. This is because it is such a relaxed enjoyable environment. It is also true that getting a potential client to commit to 30 to 45 minutes of his or her time is very difficult. So how about lunch?

Who do you invite? Anyone that could be of value to you. It's clearly a form of networking, but pick your lunch dates carefully so they truly add value. Here are some ideas.

A client from your target niche

When you take a client to lunch from your target group, the conversation will invariably include how you are both doing. When it comes to how you are doing, suggest that it would be great to have more clients in their field or in another particular field you are after.

For example, say things like, "I'd love to have more clients in your industry. Who would you work with or consider not being a direct competitor?" When they answer then you ask if there is any chance of an introduction. But don't do this right away. Spend time building up knowledge of how their industry works so you have increased knowledge for approaching others in that industry. Don't do this secretly, have your motives out in the open.

You may take them to lunch because you know that they have friends or associates in your target niche, even though they are not in it themselves. For example you might say, "Actually, I'd love to have a car dealer as a client. I've recently helped someone in a business with a similar company structure and know that I could do a lot for a car dealer." That's all you have to say – no request for a name, just seed the client's mind with the idea of who you could be of value to. They may spontaneously offer a name but it's far more likely that they will contact you in the future with a name. Or you could bring it up again at the next client meeting as you have already broken the ice on the subject.

The clients you choose to take to lunch are your better clients, obviously, so the rapport is assumed to be quite good before you even sit down to eat. For this reason you are unlikely to offend and very likely to get straight honest answers.

Other worthwhile lunch dates

Don't just stick to the obvious people, like good clients. Think laterally about who could influence others to use your services. Here are some examples that may not readily come to mind:
- Your own accountant or solicitor
- The appropriate reporter from your local paper
- Your own PA. Never underestimate PAs
- Someone you met at a function or on a flight. You may have swapped business cards so give him/her a call (or send an email) and say, 'enjoyed our conversation the other day – how are you placed for lunch or coffee on…"
- A non-competing professional you have always wanted to meet. Phone them and say something like, 'wouldn't mind catching up, it could be we have clients or prospects in common'
- A work colleague. It is rare to get one-on-ones with other key members of your firm unless you arrange it. Ask them for coffee or lunch
- Seminar presenters. You're listening to excellent stuff at times, so why not call them afterwards and get some consulting time for next to nothing by offering to take them to lunch. I have done this – it works! Note: Do not spend the entire lunch grilling them for free information. Be genuine; only ask perhaps two key questions.
- Clients you haven't seen for a while
- Clients you see frequently
- People on your "I'd love to meet them"
- The proprietor of the business next to yours

Setting a goal of just one significant lunch a week – or breakfasts which don't cut into the work day – is entirely realistic. Make up a list of 15 people that could be regarded as desirable business relationships. You could tell them right up front that you are keen to do more with their industry, so ask how is it structured, who are the key players and the main industry organisation, the most read publications, issues facing the industry. Don't overdo it, but most people enjoy having their opinion asked, so few will hold back. The goal is to go away with a much better idea about how to approach the niche you are after, not to clinch a deal that day.

It's a small world after all

How many times have you been at a party and met someone for the first time, only to discover that you have a close mutual friend, or even a relative? It always seems such a coincidence and invariably one of you will say, "Wow, it's such a small world!" No it isn't – the reason for this is that we move in surprisingly small circles but this also presents a huge opportunity.

Let me prove a couple of points to you. First, make a list of 30 friends (count couples as 1) and alongside each list, write down how or through whom you first got to meet them. This will show up a surprise, being that a very small number of people (perhaps as few as three or four) will have been responsible for introducing you to all the rest of the list!

One of the reasons for the "small world" is that you really only hang around with similar people to yourself, who in turn know others of a similar type. But, the main reason is that you have key people in your lives that know lots and lots of people. Colloquially they are known as 'connectors'.

You already know almost all of the people you need to know to build solid and abundant referrals. Go through your top 30 clients and do the same exercise as for your friends above. Identify through whom you first got to meet them. You will find that most of them became clients via a very small number of referral sources.

Six degrees of separation

An experiment was conducted in the late 1960s whereby a psychologist sent packages to 160 people at random in the state of Nebraska. He asked them to send the package to a stockbroker in Boston (about 1,200 kilometres as the crow flies) – but only via people they knew who might know the stockbroker. For example, they might have a cousin in Boston who might know of him since they are local. Or they might have a stockbroker friend in Nebraska who may know another broker in Boston who he could send it to who in turn might know a broker in the same firm who in turn knows the broker in question.

The fascinating thing was that all the packages arrived to the right person and the average number of people whose hands it passed through was between five and six, with some only going through two pairs of hands. This is where the term 'six degrees of separation' came from.

The concept of 'six degrees of separation' is that anybody chosen at random anywhere on Earth, is only separated from any other person, chosen at random, by six other people. Considering that the population of the world is more than six Billion, this appears to be almost impossible odds – yet it has been proven to be true time and time again, by people trying to disprove it.

Making the 'six degrees' work for you

Do you want a particular person as a client? Think about whom they might know and how that person may be connected to someone that you know. Depending on where you live, it may be only 2 or 3 people in the chain, rather than 6. There are web sites that do this for you. They include **www.eacademy.com** and **www.linkedin.com** which allow you to enter your profile and then through other members you may be surprised how close you are to your chosen target. The people in-between can introduce you.

How do you pay for a referral?

So you get referrals from clients and friends. Do you reward the referrer? Yes, because a reward tangibly recognises the effort of the referrer to your revenue and encourages them to do it again. US research house Cheskin Research found that the reward should not be the reason for the referral, but viewed as an appreciation on your part for genuine referrals. Overly generous gifts in fact destroy credibility in this service.

Keep the rules simple, but honest. You must fundamentally believe in the referrer's honest attempt to give you business. Some professionals only pay out when business is signed, rather than just when they are referred. If you do this, you are not recognising the part the referrer really plays in the process. They can get the prospective client to phone you and meet with you but since they cannot control the decision to actually buy, the reward should not be based on a sale.

Keep the time between the referral and giving the reward relatively short. You might want to wait until the client interview has been confirmed, but then send the gift straight after that.

What do you send? Giving a bottle of wine has become a little clichéd so has lost some of its impact – unless you know that they enjoy wine of course. It would be better to look for alternatives that don't cost much but have a high-perceived value. Possibilities include movie ticket vouchers, a cake, champagne, theatre or sports match tickets, books, coffee plunger/cups, gift baskets and pot plants. Avoid items printed with your brand and do not send cash.

An interesting approach is to ask the client what they would like. You could send them a thank you letter with a tick-the-box list asking them to "Please choose one of the following to show my appreciation and email or fax back your selection".

Referrals are the life-blood of many professional service firms, yet few have a thought-through recognition and reward system. Take the time to put one together with your team and ensure that all in the office know how it works and what their part in it is.

A subtle – yet surprisingly effective way

Put a written request in your client newsletters. There are a number of ways to word this, popular ones which have been known to work are:

> *I am delighted to say that most of my new clients are referrals from existing clients. So if you are happy with what I have been able to do for you, I would appreciate it if you passed my name onto friends and colleagues.*

We have active plans to grow within your industry next year, so if you know any other businesses like yours that may benefit from our services, please let us know.

To date our growth has primarily been in the central region, with a few clients joining us recently from the north. We wish to grow this number in the north, so if you know others like yourself in that region, please let us know.

Put a small paragraph like these at the bottom of the back page of your newsletter. While the referrals will not flood in as a result, it is a reminder to clients that referrals work for you and you are likely to want quality not quantity anyway.

Chapter 16
Referrals from other professional service firms

Find non-competing professionals with the same type of clientbase

When you know the niche you are targeting or the specific types of clients you want, you will also discover that you are not the only one wanting them. There will be other non-competing, complimentary service professionals out there who would love to have them as clients as well.

Once you have your target niche identified, make up a list of other professionals that they would logically also have advising them. How you then go about achieving these is the subject of this chapter. Note that this is harder than getting clients to refer you business.

The reasons are complicated, but will be revealed as you read the following sections.

He asked himself who influences his clients – and then had breakfast!

A building contractor analysed where his clients had come from over the previous two years. He discovered that it was NOT from advertising or directory listings as he might have thought. It was from recommendations from architects, clients, building inspectors, his sub-contractors and engineers.

So he started a series of weekly breakfasts, to which he invited the group listed above, two or three at a time. His own team are also invited and it's a very casual affair for just an hour from 7:30 to 8:30.

The impact was slow to start with but grew to be so successful that within one year he doubled his business! The people invited to the breakfasts enjoy meeting the crew and others in the industry and his team enjoy a free feed on the boss – and starting work onsite an hour later than normal.

An unexpected bonus was that productivity has increased, the relationship with existing clients has improved and his competitors have yet to work out how he does it!

Form a 'Tight Five'

This is a very powerful technique used by many professionals to grow their businesses. The principle is to find three or four non-competing professionals and meet regularly to refer clients to each other and to bounce ideas off.

The first step is to list a few other professionals that your desired target clients might also use. This is best explained using an example. Let's say you are a lawyer who wants more franchise and licensing work. Target clients are therefore businesses that are looking to sell distribution rights offshore, those that wish to franchise within the country, and online businesses with affiliate links on the site. Such businesses also require an accountant, so you phone one that you know who also works with a franchise group. The two of you meet and agree to pursue this and think that a business broker who specialises in franchises would be a good addition. So you contact one that you have heard of. The three of you meet and the business broker says he heard a brilliant speaker/consultant at a conference recently who would add marketing knowledge to the group.

See how it works? You meet at regular intervals and discuss industry issues, trends, explain how you can help your chosen target market for the benefit of the others and jointly target specific prospects. Here are a few guidelines for the successful formation and participation in a Tight Five:

- This is not a free for all and a swap of client lists. It works best when you form it to target a very specific industry, demographic or type of client that you can all benefit from.

- Think laterally when it comes to choosing 'Tight Five" members to add to your group. Start with your target market and then ask yourself what other professionals they would be likely to have in their lives.

- Meet regularly – four to six weekly – and don't miss a meeting. Some meetings will be highly productive and others disappointing, but the big hits will come over time, not immediately.

- Have a specific goal for say 12 months from when you start, such as one new franchise group that you all work with, or one new industry or a single large client.

Other ways to make them work could include a joint website if appropriate, articles in each other's newsletters, mutual links on each other's web sites, joint proposals to firms and even mentions on business cards.

They don't know what you do – and worse, they may HATE what you do!

I have run focus groups for various professional firms. While the focus groups of clients were revealing as to attitudes and meeting client expectations, when other professionals were the audience the results were rather surprising.

Many understand the basic service you offer but have their own slant on it, which could be creating quite a problem in terms of getting referrals. For example, comments from accountants in a focus group for financial planners, uncovered attitudes like, "Those guys give me the screamers – they are not true professionals in the sense that we are, they are just glorified commission salespeople." "These managed funds are alright if you don't want a good return, but I tell my clients that property is the only investment that really counts." It's fair to say that there is a fair bit of work to do with these professionals before any referrals will be coming along.

A focus group of builders for an architectural firm revealed statements like, "They build monuments to themselves and ignore the client's wishes." "I thought that architect firm designed schools, what are they doing designing houses?" Clearly with these sorts of comments there is a fair bit of educating to do. They may be 'professionals' but in most cases they know less about what you do than your average client. They will tell you that they do know, but my research tells me that it's all assumption.

What is the answer? Educate them. Taking them to lunch, and sending your newsletters will only go a small part of the way. A more effective way is to jointly meet with the client. Arranging a client meeting with another professional present allows them to see what you can do firsthand.

Keep the third party informed

If you want referrals from your alliances, you must prove that you can be of real value to their clients. Ideally, that means joint meetings as mentioned above, but this will not always be possible, of course. So, the next best thing is to keep them completely up to date with what you are doing with the client.

If whatever you are doing with the client has financial implications, offer to send a copy of relevant documents to their accountant, if legal implications, then offer to send copies to their lawyer. Offer to meet with the lawyer or account (with the client of course). Keeping the third party in the loop is critical to any long-term relationship with the third party.

WIIFT – What's In It For THEM?

Think through what the other professional will get out of the relationship. While doing the right thing for the client will be among their motives, the arrangement should be a genuine two-way street; after all they are in business too. There are many ways to do this. The obvious one is to carry their business cards and give client referrals in return. But there are other ways like the one below.

Joint seminars

One idea is that each of three professionals (you plus two others) invites 20 clients each. You all present (or you get someone to do so on your behalf) for say 20 minutes each on a themed topic, so it sounds in harmony. By definition two-thirds of the audience do not know you so you get 20 minutes to impress them with your knowledge on the subject. Note that these only work if you follow a series of steps. These are:

1. Be very selective in who you invite as they must be prime targets for the information you are offering. For example, you may decide to invite only farmers, or only trades people or only recent business start-ups. These don't really work when you mix up the audience too much as the message has to be too diverse and this can hurt credibility – trying to say you know too much about too many things.

2. Make sure the speeches are all linked within a common theme and, if possible, practice them to each other! I have seen these

seminars fall apart as one presenter changes direction on an irrelevant tangent or speaks for twice as long as they are suppose to or just 'wings it' and comes across as the fool. This ruins it for all the speakers.

3. Few will approach you on the night/morning to ask for your services. You must make this easy for them following the seminar. Hand out a one page flyer of bullet points for each presentation, which has the line at the bottom: "If you wish to come and see me to discuss how this relates to your circumstances, call me at..." also have a stack of your business cards at the door for them to take.

4. Email those of your own clients the following day – individually, not as a group – to thank them for attending and include the contact details of the other two professionals.

5. Have pre-written short articles for each other's newsletters, timed to go out in the two weeks following the seminar. This will reinforce the message.

Paul Watkins

Chapter 17
The not-so-final word

Being average doesn't work!

In Seth Godin's blog dated March 7th 2008, he writes:

> "I drove past a hobby shop yesterday... the (sign on the) awning said, 'Hobby Shop, Trains, R/C Models, Coffee, Lottery.' Bit by bit, on each declining day, it became easier to become more average, to add one more item, to sell a few more lottery tickets or another cup of coffee. And then, the next thing you know, there are some dusty model trains in the back and you're running a convenience store. This place, just about every place, has a shot at greatness, at becoming a destination, a place with profits and happiness and growth. Along the way, it's easy to start compromising your marketing, because it seems like in that moment, its expedient."

Don't compromise your position in the marketplace by adding extra services just because one isn't going the way you want to. Diversification is a core component of any investment strategy, but it applies to investments because you have little to no direct control over their return. Being in business is different. Even if you have multiple businesses, each one must be the BIG FISH in its field. That doesn't mean nationally, or internationally – just within the trading sphere you have chosen.

And the fastest way to do this is not to get bigger – it's to make the pond smaller. Focus, focus, focus on a single profitable market or service segment.

I wish you well in your career in professional services.

www.ingramcontent.com/pod-product-compliance
Lightning Source LLC
Chambersburg PA
CBHW051708170526
45167CB00002B/584